Cycling

Other titles in the Science Behind Sports series:

Baseball
Basketball
Cheerleading
Equestrian
Figure Skating
Football
Golf
Gymnastics
Ice Hockey
Snowboarding
Soccer
Swimming
Tennis
Track and Field
Volleyball
Wrestling

Cycling

STEPHEN CURRIE

LUCENT BOOKS
A part of Gale, Cengage Learning

GALE
CENGAGE Learning

Detroit • New York • San Francisco • New Haven, Conn • Waterville, Maine • London

LIBRARY OF CONGRESS CATALOGING-IN-PUBLICATION DATA

Currie, Stephen, 1960-
 Cycling / by Stephen Currie.
  pages cm. -- (Science behind sports)
 Includes bibliographical references and index.
 ISBN 978-1-4205-0819-2 (hardcover)
 1. Cycling--Juvenile literature. 2. Sports Sciences--Juvenile literature.
 I. Title.
 GV1043.5.C87 2014
 796.6--dc23

2013041965

Lucent Books
27500 Drake Rd
Farmington Hills MI 48331

ISBN-13: 978-1-4205-0819-2
ISBN-10: 1-4205-0819-9

Printed in the United States of America

1 2 3 4 5 6 7 18 17 16 15 14

TABLE OF CONTENTS

Foreword 6

Introduction
The Bicycle 8

Chapter 1
Force, Friction, and Forward Motion 11

Chapter 2
Stability, Steering, and Aerodynamics 24

Chapter 3
Basic Bicycle Components 37

Chapter 4
Muscles and Body Systems 52

Chapter 5
Nutrition, Training, and Injuries 65

Chapter 6
Performance-Enhancing Drugs 78

Notes 92
Glossary 95
For More Information 96
Index 98
Picture Credits 103
About the Author 104

FOREWORD

On March 21, 1970, Slovenian ski jumper Vinko Bogataj took a terrible fall while competing at the Ski-flying World Championships in Oberstdorf, West Germany. Bogataj's pinwheeling crash was caught on tape by an ABC *Wide World of Sports* film crew and eventually became synonymous with "the agony of defeat" in competitive sporting. While many viewers were transfixed by the severity of Bogataj's accident, most were not aware of the biomechanical and environmental elements behind the skier's fall—heavy snow and wind conditions that made the ramp too fast and Bogataj's inability to maintain his center of gravity and slow himself down. Bogataj's accident illustrates that, no matter how mentally and physically prepared an athlete may be, scientific principles—such as momentum, gravity, friction, and aerodynamics—always have an impact on performance.

Lucent Book's Science Behind Sports series explores these and many more scientific principles behind some of the most popular team and individual sports, including baseball, hockey, gymnastics, wrestling, swimming, and skiing. Each volume in the series focuses on one sport or group of related sports. The volumes open with a brief look at the featured sport's origins, history and changes, then move on to cover the biomechanics and physiology of playing, related health and medical concerns, and the causes and treatment of sports-related injuries.

In addition to learning about the arc behind a curve ball, the impact of centripetal force on a figure skater, or how water buoyancy helps swimmers, Science Behind Sports readers will also learn how exercise, training, warming up, and diet and nutrition directly relate to peak performance and enjoyment of the sport. Volumes may also cover why certain sports are popular, how sports function in the business world, and which hot sporting issues—sports doping and cheating, for example—are in the news.

Basic physical science concepts, such as acceleration, kinetics, torque, and velocity, are explained in an engaging and accessible manner. The full-color text is augmented by fact boxes, sidebars, photos, and detailed diagrams, charts and graphs. In addition, a subject-specific glossary, bibliography and index provide further tools for researching the sports and concepts discussed throughout Science Behind Sports.

The Bicycle

In one form or another, bicycles, also known as bikes, have existed for nearly two centuries, but not all early bicycles are easily recognizable as bicycles by modern standards. Some historians believe the first bicycle was invented in 1817, when German Karl von Drais built a wooden, two-wheeled contraption that he called a *laufmaschine* (running machine). Drais's invention had no pedals. A rider operated the machine by straddling it and then running while pushing it along the ground. To move faster, the rider lifted his feet from time to time to allow the wheels to take over.

By the 1860s bicycles had evolved to include foot pedals. Several people claimed to be the inventor of the foot pedal. Perhaps the strongest case belongs to Frenchman Pierre Lallement, who patented a pedal-driven bicycle in 1866 in the United States. By the early 1870s many bicycles were built with a bigger front wheel and were called "high-wheel bicycles" or simply "high wheelers." Many people eagerly purchased one of the new contraptions, some buying the high wheelers and others the more modern-looking cycles with wheels approximately the same size. Bicycling, it seemed, had arrived.

But after an initial burst of excitement, interest in bicycling waned. Part of the reason was the prevalence of accidents. Riders sat so far above the ground on high wheelers that even a small bump could cause them to fall 6 feet (1.8m) or more to the ground, causing significant injuries. Even more modest cycles with lower seats were prone to disaster;

indeed, bicycles of the late 1800s were often known as "bone shakers." Nor did it help that roads, especially in the United States, were poorly paved—if they were paved at all. Rutted dirt roads were extremely difficult for early bicycle riders to negotiate, and mud, ice, and standing water made navigating them even harder.

Over time, however, bicycle design improved and so did road surfaces. The early 1890s saw several notable improvements in bicycle technology, such as an air-filled tire (solid tires were commonplace in earlier bicycles, but these tended to make riding over even small obstacles difficult), a diamond-shaped frame, and a chain that connected the pedals to the rear wheel. By 1900 bicycles were popular as never before. Like today, people used them for recreation, racing, and getting to work. Bikes even played an important role in women's struggle for equality. As bicycles became increasingly safe and easy to ride, more women became riders, providing them with more freedom. In 1896 Susan B. Anthony, one of the leaders of the women's suffrage movement, said, "I think [bicycling] has done more to emancipate [free] women than anything else in the world. It gives women a feeling of freedom and self-reliance."[1]

Bicycles Today

In the twenty-first century bicycles remain extremely popular in the United States. Over one-quarter of the country's population goes for a bicycle ride at least once a year. This number includes millions of people who simply enjoy a leisurely ride in a park on a weekend. It also includes those who ride five or six times a week, commuting to work or pedaling for exercise. And it includes serious racers as well, many of them professionals eager to test their cycling skills against others.

Recognizing that cycling is good for the body and for the environment, many communities encourage bicycling. Chicago, Illinois, is one of several U.S. cities engaged in reshaping many of its streets to provide lanes reserved for cyclists. Denver, Colorado, has an extensive bicycle-sharing network, in which riders can rent bicycles for a low price from a kiosk and then return the bike when they are finished to any location they wish. In 2012 two cities in Minnesota, Minneapolis and St. Paul, launched ZAP Twin Cities, a new program that offers gift cards and bike accessories to those who regularly use bicycles to commute to work. According to ZAP Twin Cities, the program's goal is to encourage "more bike trips more often"[2].

Because bicycles are used for so many purposes, they come in a wide variety of shapes and styles. Road bikes have narrow tires and low handlebars and are ideal for riding along streets and highways. Mountain bikes have higher handlebars and thicker, knobby tires and are built for speed and for riding off-road, that is, along dirt paths and trails in the wilderness. Many bike racers ride around a wooden track; they use special track bikes designed for speed on a track. Some bikes are heavy, others light; some have many gears, others only a few. So choosing the proper bicycle depends on how the rider plans to use it and where he or she will be riding it.

Regardless of the type of bicycle, virtually all bikes operate under the same scientific principles. For instance, every bicycle is subject to the twin forces of gravitation and friction; the first of which explains why it is difficult to pedal uphill and the second of which explains why it is impossible to coast forever. Nearly every bicycle has the same general structure, including two equal-size wheels, handlebars, a set of pedals, and brakes. As different as bikes may be in their uses and appearance, they are all subject to the same science, and in this way they are all essentially the same.

CHAPTER 1

Force, Friction, and Forward Motion

The great English mathematician and physicist Sir Isaac Newton, who lived from 1642 to 1727, was one of the first Europeans to study motion from a scientific perspective. In 1687 he published many of his observations and conclusions in a book known today as *Mathematical Principles of Natural Philosophy*. In particular, Newton published three principles, or laws, that govern the way objects move. These principles describe the various forces that act on objects to cause them to begin motion, to speed up or slow down, to change direction, and to stop. Collectively they are called Newton's three laws of motion. They have been highly influential in helping scientists explain and understand the workings of the natural world.

The motion of a bicycle, like the motion of all objects, is subject to Newton's laws. Each aspect of a bicycle's movement, from starting to stopping and from going up a hill to turning around a corner, is described by one or more of these laws. Whether a cyclist is riding a road bike, a mountain bike, or a track bike and whether the rider is a seven-year-old child or an Olympic champion, the same rules apply. To understand how a bicycle moves, then, it is first necessary to understand Newton's laws of motion.

Newton's First Law

Two cyclists demonstrate aspects of Newton's first law of motion. The first cyclist's feet pushing against the pedals provide the force that results in movement; the second's foot against the ground provides the force to stop movement.

Newton's first law of motion has been stated in various ways since Newton first published it. One of the simplest versions divides all objects into two categories: objects at rest (not moving) and objects that are moving. Newton's first law says that an object at rest will stay at rest unless it is set into motion by some force strong enough to act upon it. The law goes on to say that any object that is moving will continue to move until a strong-enough force either changes its direction or stops it altogether. Moreover, a moving object will continue to move in a straight line and at a constant speed as long as a force does not affect it. In this way the first law of motion is about the effects of forces on objects.

The first law of motion is easy to see in the real world. For example, without any intervention, an armchair set on the floor will remain exactly where it is. So will a fork lying

in the middle of a table or a grain of rice sitting on a plate. Without any intervention, natural objects stay in place as well; a boulder or a tree will not move on its own. According to Newton's law, all of these objects will not move until a force acts on them.

It is easy to understand, too, what kinds of forces may set these objects in motion. A person can push an armchair across the floor and pick up a fork, causing the objects to move; the force that moves the objects comes from the person who is doing the moving. A grain of rice can be moved by a person, too, but is small and light enough that it can also be moved by lesser forces, such as an ant, a gust of wind, or the shaking of the plate. Boulders and trees can be set in motion by people as well as by natural forces, such as tornados or earthquakes.

The second category of objects in Newton's first law is about objects already in motion. Suppose a marble is set in motion, and it rolls along a wooden board. Newton's law says that the marble will continue to roll in a straight line until another force changes its path. If the board is perfectly smooth and level and not subject to wind or similar forces, the marble will indeed continue on a straight path. If the marble's path bends or curves, it is because another force, such as a person, a gust of wind, or some obstacle sitting in the marble's path, affected it.

Speed and Friction

Another part of Newton's first law states that the speed of a moving object is constant (stays the same) unless the object is affected by some force that speeds it up or slows it down. Friction is one of the most common forces that affects the speed of moving objects. A rolling marble, for example, will slow down gradually and eventually come to a complete stop because of friction. This type of force holds back the movement of an object that is rolling or sliding. It is caused by the movement of one object against another, such as the marble

Bike tires glide along an asphalt road. Although the road is relatively smooth, it produces enough friction to eventually bring the tire's movement to a stop in the absence of an opposing force, according to Newton's first law of motion.

rolling on a floor or a hockey puck sliding on a sheet of ice. Friction converts the energy of forward motion into heat, although the heat is not always measurable without special equipment. By reducing the amount of energy used for forward motion, friction invariably slows objects.

How much friction there is depends on the slipperiness of the surfaces. In the case of a hockey puck and ice, there is very little friction; the puck is smooth, the ice is even smoother, and the two barely connect as the puck slides across the ice. As a result, a hockey player, standing at one end of an ice rink, can hit a puck with very little effort, and it will still fly across the ice to other end of the rink. A marble rolling across a wooden floor is more affected by friction than a puck on ice: Even though both the marble and the floor are relatively smooth, they are not as smooth as the puck and the ice.

Balance and Bicycles

It is difficult, though not impossible, to balance a bicycle so only the base of its wheels are in contact with the ground. It is unlikely that the bike will remain upright for long without assistance. The majority of bikes come with kickstands to keep them upright when they are not being used. Another option is to prop the bikes up against a tree, fence, telephone pole or other sturdy structure.

In order to stand on their own, objects, such as bicycles, need to have solid contact points—that is, places where they rest on the ground. A chair and a car are excellent examples of highly stable objects: Each typically has four contact points with the floor or pavement.

It is generally necessary to have at least three contact points to ensure that an object is stable, but a bicycle has just two points of contact, small parts of the back and front wheels. Even with just two points of contact, it is possible for an object to be quite stable, but that usually requires large, wide points of contact, such as the two feet of a human. The two points of contact on a bicycle are simply not large enough to provide much support.

Sometimes, however, friction is so powerful that it will prevent movement altogether—or very nearly so. Objects with rough surfaces, sticky objects, and objects with extensive surfaces all tend to have high levels of friction. Sandpaper, rubber, and asphalt are all examples of high-friction materials. When these objects move across a surface, they will move more slowly than low-friction objects like marbles, and it will take more force to push them along. Steel is another high friction example; if two pieces of steel slide across each other they will most likely both come to a sudden stop.

Force and Gravity

Like all other objects, bicycles follow Newton's first law of motion. They remain still until a force is applied to them.

Cyclists experience how the force of gravity propels their movement as they ride on a downward slope.

Suppose that a rider is holding a bicycle upright and on its wheels, and the bike is absolutely motionless. The rider's feet are on the ground, and her hands are holding the handlebars. As long as no other force acts on the bike, the bike will remain exactly in its upright position. Newton's first law says that the bicycle will remain stationary until and unless the rider acts.

To move the bike, the rider has two basic choices. The first is to use her muscles. This means pushing forward and upward with one or both feet, hoisting herself into the seat as necessary and gliding forward as the bicycle begins to move. With this choice, the rider is providing the force. The harder she pushes, the more force she will generate, and the farther the bicycle will go.

The second choice is for the rider to simply let go of the bike. This involves a different force: gravity. All objects,

Potential and Kinetic Energy

Every object contains energy. This energy is divided into two different types: potential energy and kinetic energy. Potential energy is energy that is stored and not being used at a specific time. Kinetic energy is the energy of movement. Potential energy can be easily converted into kinetic energy. For example, suppose that a bowling ball is suspended from a ceiling on a rope. If the rope is cut, the potential energy stored in the bowling ball converts into kinetic energy, and the ball will fall.

Potential energy also converts into kinetic energy when a rider and bicycle begin to move. For example, suppose a rider is sitting motionless on a bicycle at the top of a hill, and their progress down the hill is prevented by the rider's friend holding the bike. Together, the motionless rider and bicycle are an example of potential energy. Now suppose that the friend releases the bike. The rider and bicycle will begin to move together down the slope of the hill. This converts potential energy into kinetic energy.

however large or small, exert a pull on the objects around them. This pull is known as gravity. In the case of ordinary objects, the gravitational pull is far too weak to be detected without special instruments. In the case of stars, planets, and other celestial objects, however, the power of gravity becomes unmistakable. Earth, for instance, has a gravitational force that is constantly pulling on objects, drawing them toward its center. In his book *Go Fly a Bike!*, author Bill Haduch explains, "Thirty-six hundred miles under your feet there's an eight-hundred-mile-wide solid ball of extremely hot metal pulling everything on Earth toward it."[3] This force keeps everything on Earth on the planet's surface. Gravity draws everything down as far as the surface. The surface then prevents objects from continuing to the planet's center. So with the second choice for moving the bike, if the rider lets go, gravity pulls the bike to the ground.

Earth's gravitational pull can also make riding a bike easier. Riding a bicycle down a slope is one way that gravity makes riding easier. For example, a rider can start the bike into motion simply by positioning it on a slope and setting the front wheel so it is pointing downhill. Hopping up on the bike, regardless of whether the rider gives a push, allows gravitational force to act on the bike. Gravity will pull the bicycle downhill, while at the same time, the rider exerts the force necessary to keep the bike upright and rolling on its wheels. This method takes advantage of the gravitational pull of the planet and saves the rider some energy.

Friction and Bicycles

Once a bicycle is in motion, the second part of Newton's first law applies: That is, the bike will keep moving in a straight line at a constant speed, until some other force slows it. If the rider does not pedal the bike, one of several things can happen. The first is that the bicycle will slow and eventually stop because of friction. Friction is in effect as long as the bicycle's tires are in contact with the pavement or the ground, which is, of course, nearly all the time. As the bicycle moves forward, then, it gradually loses momentum, because friction between the road surface and the bicycle wheels slows it down.

The amount of friction that affects an object as it moves is dependent on two main factors. The first is how smooth or rough the object is and how smooth or rough the surface is that the object is moving on. By this standard, a moving bicycle, like most objects designed to roll or spin, is not strongly affected by friction. It is true that bicycle tires are not completely smooth, and certainly many roads and most off-road paths are rough or even bouncy; but even so, the friction created by the rotation of the wheels along the road or path is not nearly enough to stop a bicycle right away.

The other main consideration in determining how quickly friction will slow a moving object is the amount of contact

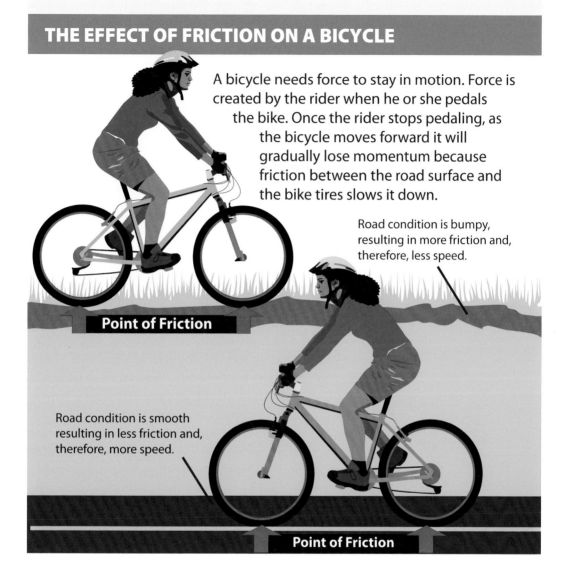

A bicycle needs force to stay in motion. Force is created by the rider when he or she pedals the bike. Once the rider stops pedaling, as the bicycle moves forward it will gradually lose momentum because friction between the road surface and the bike tires slows it down.

Road condition is bumpy, resulting in more friction and, therefore, less speed.

Point of Friction

Road condition is smooth resulting in less friction and, therefore, more speed.

Point of Friction

between the object and the surface it is moving on. The more contact there is, the more friction there will be. Consider two equally heavy boxes being dragged across the same rug. Suppose that the bottom of one of the boxes is half the size of the bottom of the other box. The box with the larger bottom, therefore, is in contact with a greater area of the rug than the box with the smaller bottom. Having less contact with the rug, the box with the smaller bottom loses less momentum due to friction as it is dragged. It moves more quickly and easily with the expense of the same amount of energy.

Similarly, bicycle wheels are designed to be less affected by friction. Bicycles have just two points of contact with the road: a small part of each wheel at any given moment. Such minimal contact between the tires and the road helps to limit the effect of friction on a moving bicycle. Bicycles with additional wheels, such as a tricycle or a child's bike with training wheels, increases the amount of friction available to bring the bike to a stop. Bicycles, then, are not subject to high levels of friction, but friction does take a toll on the speed of a bicycle.

Air Resistance

Bicycles are also affected by another force: air resistance. Air is not a visible barrier, of course, and it is easy enough to push through air under most circumstances; if it were not, motion of any kind would essentially be impossible. Nonetheless, air has power in the form of wind. And even when air is more or less motionless, it nevertheless interacts with an object traveling forward. "As you roll along," writes one cycling expert, "air molecules are slamming into you. Sure, each one is pretty light, but they add up!"[4] The constant bombardment of air molecules against a bike and its rider can slow them and eventually bring them to a stop.

Suppose, then, that a bicycle has been put into motion by a rider. Suppose, too, that the rider is coasting—that is, sitting on the bike without moving and allowing the bicycle to move under its own power. How long it will take for the bike to stop depends on a number of factors. One of these is the direction the bike is traveling: downhill, uphill, or across a level surface. A downhill slope does not reduce friction, but gravity will act to some extent to counteract the friction and allow the bicycle to travel farther than if it were moving along a level surface. In the same way, although an uphill slope does not add friction, the bike will be working against gravity and will slow more quickly than it would if it were level.

Wind speed and direction also affect the distance a coasting bicycle will travel. Traveling into the wind, with the wind

blowing directly into the cyclist's face, is much more difficult and less efficient than traveling with the wind, when the wind is blowing in the same direction that the bicycle is traveling. A cyclist coasting into a strong wind is not only fighting friction and ordinary air resistance but is also being pushed backward by the force of the breeze. He will come to a stop quite soon. In contrast a cyclist traveling with the wind can use his or her body as a sail, causing the bike to move more quickly as it coasts along.

Road Surface, Tire Pressure, and Initial Force

The surface on which a bicycle moves also plays a role in determining how far it will travel. Gravel, for instance, produces a great deal of friction, so a bicycle moving on a gravel road will slow much more quickly than it will on a paved street. The amount of air in a bike's tires also makes a difference. A tire that is not fully inflated has a greater area of contact with the roadway, creating more friction than a tire containing the maximum amount of air. This is one reason why bicycle manuals advise bike owners to keep tires fully inflated.

The major factor involved in how far a bicycle will travel, however, is the initial amount of force applied to it to set it in motion. A strong push off causes the bicycle to glide a long

Cycling on a beach is more difficult than cycling on a smooth road because of the amount of friction created by the sand.

way before friction and air resistance slow it to the point where it no longer is able to move forward. A weaker push off may still set the bike into motion, but the slower initial movement of the bike—and the smaller force used to propel it—means that the bicycle will travel a shorter distance before stopping. In other words, the impact of the forces acting to slow the bicycle will sooner or later outweigh the impact of the initial force that propelled it forward and the greater the initial force, the longer it will take.

The motion of a bicycle as a cyclist begins to ride is thus more complex than it might first appear. The speed with which the bike moves and the distance it will travel before stopping are both governed by a variety of factors. These include wind speed, tire inflation, the slope and surface of the road or trail the bike is on, and the forcefulness of the initial push off. When cyclists begin their rides, they are not just looking forward to getting exercise and enjoying the sunshine; rather, they are exemplifying some of nature's basic rules—in the form of Newton's first law of motion.

CHAPTER 2

Stability, Steering, and Aerodynamics

R iding a bicycle, including steering, stopping, and going as quickly and efficiently as possible, is fundamentally subject to scientific laws. Even the position a cyclist uses to ride is based on science. From stability to steering to aerodynamics, science determines how bicycles move and how they stop, once they have been set into motion.

Stability

Bicycles by themselves are not terribly stable; they cannot stand up without the aid of a rider; a kickstand; or an object, such as a tree, to lean against. A person riding on a bicycle is not especially stable either due to the position of the rider's center of gravity. The center of gravity for any object is the object's central point. A person on a bicycle has a very high center of gravity. Most of the weight belongs to the person rather than the bike, and the person is several feet off the ground. In general objects with a low center of gravity are more stable than objects with a high center of gravity, and a person on a bicycle is no exception.

Making a bicycle move forward, however, creates stability. There is much debate over exactly why this is so. The Exploratorium, a science museum in California, reports that

"many scientists are in complete disagreement about even the fundamentals of balancing and steering."[5] The best reason, however, involves the basic laws of motion. According to Newton's first law, an object that is moving tends not only to remain in motion, but also to continue to move in the direction it is already traveling. Once a rider has set a bike in motion, then, the bicycle's tendency to keep going forward is stronger than its tendency to become unstable. Indeed, as the rider increases his or her speed, the bike becomes ever more stable.

Balancing on a moving bike is not straightforward, however. It is an extremely complex process. As the bike moves forward, the rider makes subtle shifts in posture to prevent the bicycle from falling over. "You actually stay up and balance by twitching and wiggling your handlebars the whole time you're riding," writes author Bill Haduch in his book

Although their center of gravity is high, two women maintain stability while riding their bikes by subtly moving their handlebars and shifting their weight.

Go Fly a Bike! "You don't even know it, but when your brain senses that the bike is beginning to fall over—even the tiniest little bit—you automatically twitch the handlebars in that direction. The bike's reaction? It leans a little in the opposite direction."[6]

Riders are typically unaware of making all these delicate shifts and changes in balance. The movements are natural and unconscious; without even thinking about it, the rider knows exactly how much pressure to apply, and in which direction, to keep traveling in a straight line. In fact, some cyclists have a difficult time believing that they actually do wiggle the handlebars and shift their weight or that the bike makes small shifts to the left and right as it moves forward.

A Bike's Self-Stability

It is possible for a person to balance on a bicycle without moving. In a cycling race at the 1964 Olympic Games in Tokyo, Japan, two track riders sat perfectly still on their bikes for over twenty minutes. (Because riders expend less energy when they ride directly behind another cyclist it can often be an advantage for track riders to force their opponents to make the first move). However, few riders try to balance for long on an unmoving bike, because doing so is simply too difficult. While waiting for a red light to change on a city street, for instance, casual cyclists will typically maintain their balance by disengaging one foot from the pedals and placing it on the curb or pavement, thus introducing a third point of contact with the ground.

Although bicycles are inherently unstable when motionless, they can often remain upright as they move—even without being guided by a rider or a person's hand. This feature is known as self-stability. As the bicycle rolls forward, it automatically makes small steering adjustments to keep it in balance. In an article in *Scientific American* magazine, John Matson writes, "If a bicycle starts to tip over, its front wheel turns into the fall, bringing the bike back into balance, just as a rider would do if he or she were behind the handlebars."

Exactly why bicycles are self-stable is unclear. At one point scientists believed that it was the result of a force called gyroscopic inertia—the force that keeps a coin rolling along a tabletop or a top spinning more or less in place. Further research has demonstrated, however, that this is not the case.

John Matson. "A Bicycle Built for None." *Scientific American*, April 14, 2011. www.scientificamerican.com/article.cfm?id=self-stable-bike.

Steering and Turns

Shifts and changes in balance not only help keep riders upright; they also help cyclists steer their bicycles. Constant alterations in the way riders sit on the seat and in the direction that they tilt the handlebars can send the bicycle moving in a slightly different direction. Sometimes these shifts are intuitive. "When you turn your front wheel to the right," explains the Exploratorium, "your bike heads to the right."[7] Sometimes, however, the shifts are less intuitive. When the rider shifts his body to the left, for example, the bicycle actually responds by turning slightly to the right. Essentially, the bicycle attempts to maintain equilibrium and balance by moving in a way that makes up for the change in position of the rider.

Another example of a counterintuitive shift involves sharp turns. Many riders believe that making a sharp turn requires turning the wheel quickly to one side or the other. This is not true. "If you are traveling fast and you twist the wheel

MOMENTUM

Momentum is the product of the mass and speed of a moving object. A bike will reach different levels of momentum depending on the size of the bicycle and of the rider (mass), and the force with which he pedals (speed). In order to make a turn a rider should turn the bike's handlebars in the direction he wants to head. If the rider turns the handle bars too sharply he may fall off the bike as the momentum carries the bike to turn but the rider to continue on a straight course.

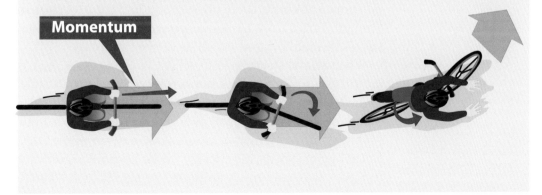

Momentum

sharply," the Exploratorium explains, "your momentum may cause you and your bicycle to part company [separate] when your bike turns and you continue in a straight course."[8] In fact, turning too suddenly can cause a bicycle to crash even if the rider can manage to stay on; the force of thrusting the front wheel in a different direction can destabilize the bike.

Mass, or the amount of matter in an object, plays a role in steering and turns as well. According to Newton's laws of motion, objects of greater mass will always respond more slowly to outside forces than objects of lesser mass. It takes less force to change the direction of a baseball than a bowling ball, for example, assuming that they are each traveling at the same speed. In cycling, then, the heavier the rider and the heavier the bicycle, the more slowly the bicycle will respond when the rider makes a turn. As a result, heavier cyclists may need to start their turns sooner than lighter ones and may even have to dismount in order to change direction while a lighter cyclist might be able to change direction while remaining on the bike.

Posture, Speed, and Aerodynamics

In general the faster a cyclist travels, the more stable the bicycle will be. Traveling fast, however, is not easy. One reason for this is friction, the energy that is lost as the bicycle's tires make contact with the trail or the road. Without friction, a bike would be able to go much faster. Another reason traveling fast is not easy is that riders provide all of a bicycle's forward motion and they are limited by their physical ability. Few people can pedal a bicycle at more than 40 miles per hour (64kmh); their bodies simply do not permit it. Strength varies from person to person, but each individual has a threshold beyond which he or she cannot go.

The main obstacle to fast cycling, however, is air. Just as air will eventually slow and stop a rider coasting on a bicycle, air also slows down a rider who is pedaling. When a rider pedals at slow speeds, such as less than 10 miles per hour (16kmh), air resistance is minimal, at least on a calm day. But at higher speeds, the effect of the air becomes significant indeed. "At twenty miles an hour," writes Haduch, "you're

CYCLING AND AERODYNAMICS

All cyclists experience air resistance when riding. Cyclists who sit in a crouch position (A) face less air resistance and, as a result, are more aerodynamic and able to move much faster. In the traditional upright position (B) cyclists face much more air resistance, which results in a slower ride.

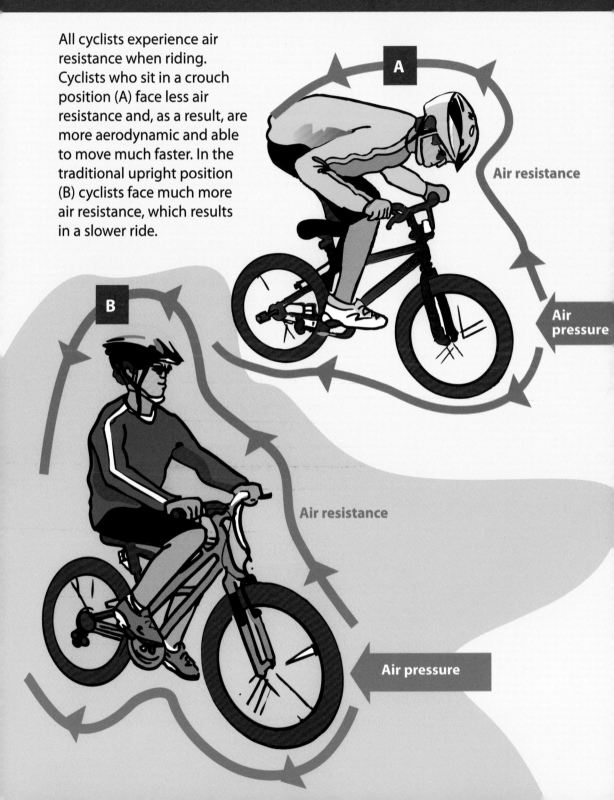

pushing aside three thousand pounds of air every three minutes!" This amount of air resistance wears down the rider and slows the bicycle. "If you're not trained for racing," Haduch adds, "just moving all this air is 90 percent of your work."[9]

Air follows certain patterns of movement; the study of these movements is known as aerodynamics. There is no way to avoid all air resistance while riding a bike, but aerodynamics can help cyclists limit the amount of resistance they face. One way to limit resistance is how a rider sits on the bike. A rider who is sitting straight up on the seat has a great deal of air to push aside while pedaling. In contrast, a rider who is leaning forward and crouching as low as possible will encounter less air and, therefore, has less air to push aside, allowing him to use less energy and go faster.

Road racers almost always use a very low crouch position as they ride. Most road bikes have downturned handlebars, which enable riders to crouch lower than with upright handlebars and helps them remain in control of the bicycle even while leaning far forward. Cyclists do need to be careful not to lean so far forward that they limit their oxygen intake, as it can be difficult to breathe deeply while crouching. Racers, therefore, need to find the best riding position for them, one that reduces the amount of air that they must push aside and that allows them to breathe as deeply as necessary.

Slowing and Stopping

A moving bicycle will eventually stop on its own because of friction, air resistance, or gravity. But riders often need to slow down or stop more quickly than friction allows. A casual cyclist who slows for a stoplight, a mountain biker who stops to avoid a downed tree, and a road racer who reduces his speed in advance of a turn will all be in trouble if they rely solely on natural forces to stop or slow their bikes. The earliest bicycles had no easy way for riders to bring them safely to a stop. The invention of brakes solved this problem.

The earliest bicycle brakes, known as plungers, were used on high wheelers. Riders operated them by means of a lever. By pushing or pulling on the lever, which was located on the handlebars, the rider could make a piece of metal located near the front wheel press tightly against the wheel. The pressure caused friction, which slowed the forward motion of the cycle; if the rider applied enough force, then the bicycle quickly came to a stop.

Unfortunately there were two significant problems with plunger brakes. For one, even though the metal pressing against the wheel effectively slowed the bike, it also caused a great deal of wear and tear to the tire and sometimes to

Early braking systems on high-wheeler bikes were known as plungers.

Aviation and Bikes

Most people know that brothers Orville and Wilbur Wright built the first successful motor-powered airplane. Their first flight took place near Kitty Hawk, North Carolina, in December 1903. It is less well-known that the Wrights became involved in aviation through an interest in bicycles. In 1892 they opened their own bicycle shop, where they built and repaired bikes.

Today, the link between bikes and aviation is not at all obvious. Bicycles, after all, are small and run on human power; airplanes are enormous and run on jet fuel. But in the Wrights' time there was a clear connection. Firstly, riding a bicycle and piloting a small airplane both rely heavily on balance. Secondly, designers of bicycles and designers of airplanes all have to address air resistance and use aerodynamics. Thirdly, early bicycles and airplanes needed to be strong yet lightweight. The Wrights' work with bicycles gave them plenty of hands-on experience with aerodynamics and building materials that proved invaluable in helping them construct the world's first motor-powered flying machine.

the metal. Over time the tire deteriorated and lowered the braking power of the plunger. The other problem was that the plunger worked very poorly when wet. As the Exploratorium explains, "water decreases the friction between the [metal] and the tire, lessening the braking power."[10] Since the tire was constantly wet on rainy days or when streets were covered with standing water, the friction was continually being compromised, making it dangerous to ride a bike with a plunger braking system.

Coaster Brakes

In the 1890s a new bicycle braking system known as coaster brakes became increasingly common on bikes, especially as high wheelers disappeared and bikes with equal-size wheels became the standard. Coaster brakes are also known

as back-pedaling brakes or foot brakes, and riders operate them by pedaling backward. Coaster brakes are built inside the rear hub, or assembly, of the bicycle, and they work by applying friction to the axle of the wheel.

Riders of bikes with coaster brakes simply pedal backwards in order to come to a stop.

Coaster brakes have several important advantages over plunger brakes. Because coaster brakes use plenty of grease, they do not wear out easily, and they work just fine when wet. "Coaster brakes are unaffected by weather," explains bicycle expert Sheldon Brown. "They work just as well in the rain as they do in dry conditions."[11] Coaster brakes also require very little strength or coordination to apply, which makes them excellent for elderly or infirm people who would prefer not to give up riding altogether. Another advantage is that coaster brakes need virtually no maintenance.

Still, coaster brakes are far from perfect. For serious riders, the biggest issue is that they cannot be used with certain kinds of gearing systems, making them unavailable for use on most highly sophisticated bikes. Coaster brakes are also potentially dangerous. Although they do not wear out, they can become suddenly ineffective, because they rely on a working chain to stop the bike. According to Frank Rowland Whitt and David Gordon Wilson, authors of the book, *Bicycling Science*, "if the chain breaks or comes off the sprockets there is no braking at all."[12] And like plunger brakes, coaster brakes are designed to work on only one wheel. There is no backup if that single brake fails.

Rim Brakes

The most popular and familiar kind of brake used for modern bicycles is the rim brake. Rim brakes consist of two pads, usually made of rubber, that are attached to a metal housing near the top of the wheel. Unlike plunger brakes and

A lever on the handlebar is used to activate rim brakes, which are made of pads that are positioned on either side of the front and rear wheels.

coaster brakes, rim brakes are attached to both the rear and front wheels. They are positioned so that one pad is on each side of each wheel. Cables connect the pads and the housing to two levers, one mounted just below each handlebar. When the rider squeezes the levers, the pads press against the metal rims of the wheels and grip them. Squeezing the brake levers quickly and tightly will stop the bicycle more or less immediately; squeezing the levers lightly adds friction and slows the bike without stopping it.

Rim brakes are generally very effective. They are lightweight, reliable, and powerful. Like other brake types, however, they do have some drawbacks. The braking power of rim brakes under wet conditions is about one-tenth the power of the brakes on dry roads. The frequent pressure of the rubber pads against the metal of the wheel rim eventually damages the rubber, although replacing the pads is easy and can be done quickly. Another problem with rim brakes is that they can move out of alignment, meaning that when the rider squeezes the levers, the brakes do not grab the right places on the rims. Most riders find, however, that a quick brake check before riding, with adjustments as needed, will keep rim brakes in good working order.

Using the brakes involves science, too. Suppose a rider needs to bring his bike to a sudden stop. Given the speed at which he is going and the surface on which he is traveling, it is possible to estimate the distance the bicycle will need to stop. On dry concrete, for instance, a rider traveling at 10 miles per hour (16kmh) will be able to stop in less than 4 feet (1.2m). On ice, it will take a rider almost 30 feet (9.1m) to come to a stop. Going faster on any surface increases the stopping distance, sometimes dramatically. A rider traveling at 20 miles per hour (32kmh) will continue another 15 feet (4.6m) before stopping on dry pavement; on ice, it will take 115 feet (35m).

Most cyclists use their own riding experience to know

when—and how hard—to apply the brakes. In most circumstances it is wise to brake when the pavement or trail ahead seems to have obstacles or sharp turns that should be approached with caution. "If I'm coming into a sharp corner I'll brake ahead of the corner," says American racer Ruthie Matthes, "and as I'm going into the corner [I] release the front brake and only use the rear brake."[13] Usually, though, it is advisable to brake slowly and gently rather than jamming on the brakes as hard as possible. Braking slowly allows the rider to maintain more control over the bicycle and reduces the possibility of a crash.

Even though most cyclists do not know all the science behind bicycling when they go for a ride, they still make use of the scientific principles. Even if they cannot articulate what they are doing or why they are doing it, riders consistently wiggle their hands on the handlebars as they ride, seeking better stability, and they unconsciously start their turns and put on the brakes at appropriate moments, neither too early nor too late. Over time, too, many riders realize that they can travel faster and more efficiently if they crouch as they pedal. In a way, then, the science behind cycling is just common sense.

CHAPTER 3

Basic Bicycle Components

From a mechanical perspective, few of the parts that make up a bicycle are necessary for the function of the bike. It is perfectly possible to ride a bike without mudguards, rear reflectors, or a seat. It is even possible to ride without brakes or handlebars. Indeed, a bike needs only a handful of components to function, and they include a frame, wheels, pedals, and chain. These components are basic to the construction of nearly every modern bicycle.

The Frame

The design of a bicycle begins with the frame, or the network of metal pieces on which the wheels, seat, and pedals are supported. The frame, therefore, is fundamental to the rest of the machine. "The frame," writes bicycle enthusiast Robert Penn in his book, *It's All About the Bike*, "is the soul of the bicycle."[14]

There are several basic requirements for a frame. Most importantly the frame must be strong. A bicycle frame holds not only the seat and the handlebars but also a rider, so it must be sturdy enough to carry the weight of these parts and the rider. Moreover, bicycles are subjected to other forces, such as quick stops, rapid turns, and the bouncing of the

The frame of a bike must be both strong and flexible in order to withstand the stress of a rider's movement and the impact of the trail or road.

wheels on the ground. If the frame is not sufficiently sturdy, the bicycle will break when impacted by these forces.

Frame strength is measured in part by ultimate tensile stress (UTS), which is the greatest force the frame can withstand without snapping. Frame strength is also measured by fatigue-limit stress, which is how long a frame will last under normal use before it fails. All metals fatigue, or grow weaker, with use and with time; indeed, the greatest threat to a bicycle frame is not the sudden stress of an abrupt stop or other maneuver but the gradual wear and tear on the metal over time. Some experts argue that fatigue-limit stress is the single most important factor in building a strong bicycle frame. "The fatigue-limit stress rather than the ultimate tensile stress should be used as a [primary] criterion of acceptable strength,"[15] write Frank Rowland Whitt and David Gordon Wilson in their book, *Bicycling Science*.

Finding the Right Frame

In his book, *It's All About the Bike*, Robert Penn describes how science can be used to find the best possible frame for a particular rider. He writes,

A . . . reliable fitting or sizing method . . . is to take body measurements and interpret them into a frame size. Inside leg (crotch to floor), torso, arm, femur, forearm, shoulder width, shoe-size, height and weight all go into the analysis. In this way, the experience of the person doing the fitting and designing of the frame is . . . crucial.

Today, for both professional athletes and amateur riders with deep pockets [enough money], there are various high-tech fitting methods that entail a scientific approach to the biomechanics of cycling. They involve motion capture systems that process data taken from anatomical points [places on the body] on the rider, providing a real-time view of the riding position and pedal action at different workloads. The rider being fitted usually sits on an adjustable jig or "size-cycle," a simple frame mounted on a machine that provides traction when you pedal.

Robert Penn. *It's All About the Bike*. New York: Bloomsbury, 2010, p. 21.

The strength of a bicycle frame is closely related to its flexibility. A completely rigid frame might seem ideal from a strength perspective, but it is not because a sudden force applied to a rigid frame is likely to break the metal. The best frame, actually, has significant flexibility. When a flexible frame is stressed—for instance, when the bicycle bounces on pavement—it will bend or stretch slightly before resuming its original shape. The movement is too small and swift to be seen with the eye, but it is essential for absorbing the stress and protecting the bike from damage.

In addition to being strong and flexible, a bicycle frame should also be lightweight. This is particularly true for bicycles designed for speed. In their book, *The Ultimate Bicycle Book*, authors Richard Ballantine and Richard Grant write, "The better the bike, the less there is of it."[16] A heavy frame creates a heavy bicycle, and a heavy bicycle is difficult to pedal, quickly resulting in a tired cyclist.

Materials

Most bicycle frames today are made from steel or a combination of iron and several other elements. Easy to obtain

THE COMPONENTS OF A BICYCLE

The basic components of every modern bicycle include a frame, wheels, pedals, and a chain.

Saddle area:
saddle
seat post

Front set:
handlebar grip
head tube
shock absorber
front brakes
fork

Frame:
top tube
down tube
seat tube
seat stay
chain stay

Wheel:
spokes
hub
rim
tire
valve

rear brakes
cogset
rear derailleur

pedal
crank arm

front derailleur
chain
chain rings

and relatively inexpensive to buy, steel is stronger and more flexible than most other metals. It also has high UTS, which means it is difficult to break. Steel can be more easily repaired than many other metals, too, and it is known for its durability. "Years of riding left in them," says one mechanic about steel-frame bikes. "We have a near constant supply of steel frames in for restoration. Many are over fifty years old."[17]

The major drawback to steel is weight. Consequently, some riders prefer frames made from aluminum, which are not quite as strong or durable as steel but are usually much lighter. Unfortunately aluminum does not flex well. "The more it gets to bend," says the Exploratorium, a science museum in California, "the quicker it reaches the end of its life."[18] Aluminum bikes are sometimes built with thicker frames than steel bicycles, in order to limit the amount of flexing the metal must undergo. Even so, the lack of flexibility in aluminum frames is an issue for many riders.

Given the problems with steel and aluminum, some professional cyclists favor bike frames made of other materials. Some riders choose frames made from titanium, which is stronger than either steel or aluminum, and it weighs less. Other riders use a nonmetal substance known as carbon fiber, which is extremely flexible and also quite light. Unfortunately both titanium and carbon fiber are expensive, and carbon fiber is often at risk of cracking; even the act of tightening a carbon fiber tube may destroy it.

Triangles and Trusses

The design of a bicycle frame is also important in keeping a bicycle steady and strong. The frame of most bicycles is in the shape of two triangles. The forward triangle is located in the center of the bike, between and above the two wheels. One side of this triangle is known as the top tube. It extends from just below the handlebars in the front of the bike to just below the seat in the center. The top tube is generally horizontal, although on mountain bikes, in particular, it can slope downward from the handlebars toward the seat.

The second side of the triangle, the seat tube, runs not quite vertically downward from just below the seat. The

Bike frames can typically be broken down into a series of interconnected triangles that form a truss-like structure that is strong and stable.

bottom of the seat tube ends near the pedals, at a part of the bike often called the bottom bracket. The third side, the down tube, completes the figure by running diagonally from the bottom bracket up to a point near the handlebars. The triangle is not equilateral, in which all sides are the same length and all angles have the same degree measure; but the seat tube and the top tube are often close to the same length.

The second triangle is more difficult to perceive if the wheels are on the bike, but with the rear wheel and chain removed, it is much easier to spot. The seat tube is at the front of the figure. The other two sides of the triangle stretch from the back wheel to the top and bottom of the seat tube; the top one is sometimes called the seat stay and the bottom one the chain stay. The two triangles therefore form a sort of diamond with the seat tube dividing it roughly in half. The resulting figure is often called a diamond frame, and the vast majority of bikes built today use this design. According to the Exploratorium, "the design has changed very little since . . . the 1880s."[19]

The diamond frame is based on a structure known as the truss, a series of interconnected triangles. Many bridges use a truss design; the Eiffel Tower in Paris, France, is probably the single most famous example of a truss building. Trusses are noted for their stability and strength. The vertices of a triangle, or the places where the sides meet, are fixed in position; they cannot move relative to each other unless the lengths of the sides change. Thus, if force is applied to one side or vertex of the figure, it is typically absorbed without deforming the shape. This is not the case for shapes such as squares or pentagons, where the vertices can move more freely.

Bike wheels come in many varieties, but all consist of an outer rim, usually made from an aluminum alloy, with an axle at the center around which the rim rotates.

Wheels

Wheels are also vital to bicycle function. Indeed, the word *bicycle* comes from the prefix *bi-*, meaning two, and the root word *cycle*, or wheel. There are different kinds of bicycle

wheels because there are different types of bikes, such as track bikes, mountain bikes, and road bikes. For example, track bikes have skinnier wheels than mountain bikes, and mountain bikes have wheels that typically have a smaller radius than those of road bikes. Still, every bicycle has two wheels and without them the bicycle would be unable to move.

Like bicycle frames, bicycle wheels are exceptionally well designed for stability and speed. Ballantine and Grant write, "A bicycle wheel is one of the strongest engineering structures in the world."[20] While bicycle wheels are very light, rarely weighing more than 5 pounds (2.3kg), they are designed to withstand enormous stress. Not only do they rotate at high speeds, but they are also built to withstand sudden turns and stops, and they support both the weight of the bicycle and the weight of the rider.

Cadence

A cyclist's cadence is how fast he or she pedals. Most experts advise riders to find a comfortable cadence and stick to it as much as possible, especially when turning into the wind or riding uphill. Instead of lowering their cadence to make pedaling easier, riders should maintain it by gearing down, or reducing the gear they are using. Keeping a steady cadence allows the rider to use less energy in the long run.

For some riders, a comfortable cadence may mean a fairly leisurely 60 pedal rotations a minute. At this rate each foot goes around once every second. Other riders are more comfortable and efficient at a slightly higher cadence, perhaps 75 or 90 rotations per minute. Road racers sometimes go much faster, occasionally reaching rates of 120 rotations a minute or even more. Obviously, conditions affect a rider's cadence; when a cyclist slows to avoid a pothole or some other obstacle, for instance, the cadence is likely to go down temporarily. However, riders tend to be best off when they maintain a consistent cadence whenever possible.

A bicycle wheel consists of several parts. The outside is called the rim; this is the hoop-like part that rotates when the wheel spins. Until the 1980s, steel was the most common material used for wheel rims, and while some rims continue to be made from steel, today most rims are made from an aluminum alloy in order to pair lightness with strength as cheaply as possible. The center of the wheel, known as the hub, contains an axle, a small horizontal piece of metal around which the rest of the wheel revolves. Hubs also include ball bearings, which permit the wheel to rotate freely around the axle.

Spokes, Tubes, and Tires

To form a wheel, the hub and the rim must be connected, and in nearly all bicycle wheels they are connected by spokes. Spokes are long, rigid pieces of metal that run from the hub

A cyclist repairs the inner tube of one of his tires, which holds pressurized air that absorbs the shock of bumps and bounces during a ride.

outward to the rim. The number of spokes a wheel has varies. More spokes support the wheel rim better, but fewer spokes result in a lighter bicycle. Since saving weight is paramount in bicycle racing, bicycles used for racing generally make do with wheels that have fewer spokes. A standard bike might have thirty-two-spoke wheels, for instance, but racers often choose bicycle wheels with twenty-two, twenty, or even sixteen spokes.

Although sturdy, spokes are lightweight and easily maneuverable. Wheels built with spokes are especially useful in making turns. The rider can change the position of a spoked wheel with little resistance from the surrounding air, which flows smoothly through the empty spaces between the spokes. The light weight of the spokes also aids in acceleration and in climbing hills. Spoked wheels are not the only choice, however, and some bikes have solid wheels, called disc wheels. Many cyclists prefer disc wheels for indoor races, where winds and hills are of no concern and spokes provide less benefit.

All bicycle wheels also include an inflatable rubber tube that curls around the rim and is packed with air under pressure. The flexibility of the tube preserves the integrity of the metal rim and protects the bicycle and the rider from the full effect of bumps and bounces. The tube is encased in a rubber tire, which grips both sides of the rim and holds it in place.

Pedals

The wheels of a bicycle are propelled by the pedals. Bicycles have two pedals, which are rotated by the rider's feet. The pedals function as a crank, a device that rotates again and again to move an object. The rotation of the crank is called circular motion. It is produced by a repetitive movement that is often called reciprocation or reciprocating motion. In the case of a bicycle, the reciprocating motion is the constant up-and-down movement of the rider's feet. This energy is then converted into the circular motion of the pedals.

A bike's pedals function as a type of crank, and the reciprocating motion of the rider's feet propels the bike forward.

While many cranks have just one shaft, or arm, bicycle pedal systems have two, and both pedals are used to produce the desired circular motion. The two pedals are connected by a zigzagged shaft that keeps the pedals positioned opposite each other. When one of the pedals is up, the other is down, and when one pedal is in front, the other is behind. This means the rider must use an eggbeater pedaling motion in which the feet move one after the other.

Converting the up-and-down reciprocation of the rider's feet to the circular motion of the pedals is only part of the process. The next step is to convert the circular motion to the forward motion necessary to propel the bicycle. This is done by linking the pedals to one of the wheels. When the pedals on a bicycle are turned, the wheel connected to the pedals automatically spins and moves the bicycle forward. The other wheel is not connected to the pedals and does not move on its own. Instead, it moves only because the other wheel is moving.

Chains

The simplest way to convert the force of bicycle pedals into forward motion is to mount the pedals directly on one of the wheels of the bicycle. On many early bicycles the pedals were attached to the center of the front wheel. This design

A bike's pedals are connected to the rear wheel by a circular chain, which transfers the energy created when the rider moves the pedals to the wheel, propelling the bike forward.

is known as front-wheel drive. However, these front-wheel drive bicycles had a significant problem. A single rotation of the pedals on these bikes resulted in the front wheel making one complete rotation. The distance traveled was therefore dependent on the wheel's circumference. A standard-size wheel, which had a circumference of about 6 feet (1.8m), was inefficient with front-wheel drive; the distance traveled with one rotation was no more than the few feet.

The answer, then, was to use a wheel as large as possible. A wheel 6 feet in diameter (1.8m) has a circumference of about 19 feet (5.8m), meaning that a bicycle with the pedals mounted on a wheel of this size will travel about three times farther with a single pedal stroke than it would with a standard-size wheel. Early bicycles that utilized front-wheel drive often had wheels of this size. Unfortunately because riders were seated so high up, they often fell, resulting in serious injury. As a result, reckless young men were usually the only ones to ride such bikes.

The modern-day system for converting circular motion to forward motion does not use pedals directly on a wheel. Instead, the pedals are typically connected to a continuous chain, several feet long, that links the pedals to the rear wheel. The chain transfers the energy from the pedals to the back wheel, propelling that wheel forward. As the pedals turn faster, the chain moves more rapidly as well, increasing the rear wheel's speed of rotation and making the bike move forward at a faster pace.

Gears

Bicycle chains also allow for gearing. Nearly all bicycles today come with multiple gears. The chain wraps around two sets of toothed gears, known as sprockets. One of these sprocket sets is connected to the pedals. The other is located at the junction of the chain and the bicycle's rear wheel. The set in the front usually has two or three different sprockets

BICYCLE CHAIN AND GEARS

Bicycle chains allow for the conversion of circular motion to forward motion, as well as allow the rider to adjust the bike to different gears.

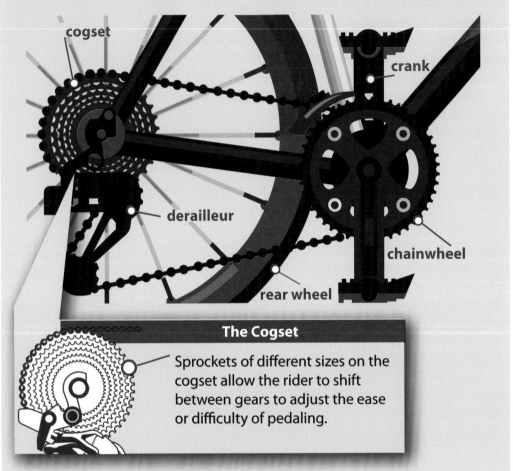

cogset

crank

derailleur

chainwheel

rear wheel

The Cogset

Sprockets of different sizes on the cogset allow the rider to shift between gears to adjust the ease or difficulty of pedaling.

of different sizes; the one in the back may have seven or more. By using levers called shifters that are attached to the handlebars, the rider can make the chain travel across different combinations of sprockets. This process is called shifting gears.

Cyclists can adjust the gears they use to best suit riding conditions. When pedaling uphill, the cyclist can simply downshift, which moves the chain to a combination of sprockets that makes pedaling easier. Downshifting reduces the power of each pedal stroke, but it is a reasonable trade-off for easier pedaling. By shifting gears, a rider can save valuable energy while going uphill, yet still keep the rear wheel moving at a reasonable rate. The gears can also be adjusted to make pedaling harder (such as when traveling downhill or with the wind), providing more force with each pedal stroke and increasing the speed of the bicycle. Through the use of gears, then, pedaling can be made as efficient as possible for the circumstances.

The frame, wheels, pedals, and chain together make a bicycle what it is. Through the 1800s, inventors created a highly efficient design and system of propulsion, allowing bicycle riders to move quickly and easily across the ground. Penn writes, "The bicycle can be ridden, on a reasonable surface, at four or five times the pace of walking, with the same amount of effort—making it the most efficient, self-powered means of transportation ever invented."[21]

CHAPTER 4

Muscles and Body Systems

C ycling, as with all other sports, requires a person to use a combination of muscles and body systems in order to participate. The muscles and body systems needed vary depending on the sport. In baseball, for example, players need strong arms, shoulders, and backs, whereas in running, sprinters need very powerful legs. Similarly, gymnasts generally need a better sense of balance than swimmers, and distance runners need significantly more lung power than golfers.

At the same time, even the parts of the body not obviously used by an athlete are often more important than they seem. To draw maximum benefit from their arm and shoulder strength, for instance, baseball players need to develop their leg muscles as well, and sprinters' upper bodies are often nearly as powerful as their legs. And while an excellent pair of lungs is a requirement for endurance sports, such as cross-country skiing and distance running, athletes in other sports, such as football and figure skating, also benefit from increasing their lung capacity.

In addition to developing the particular muscles or body systems that aid them most in their sport, responsible athletes also pay attention to their overall physical fitness. Even the best athletes cannot perform at their best if they are sick, tired, overweight, or underweight.

Strong Arms and Shoulders

Among the muscle groups that are more important to cyclists than they seem at first are the arms and the shoulders. Compared to sports such as tennis and baseball, of course, the value of the arms and the shoulders in cycling is low. It is possible to be an excellent cyclist even with below-average arm and shoulder strength. When riding, after all, the arms and shoulders remain basically immobile most of the time. There is no repetitive pulling motion as there is in swimming, no throwing movement as in baseball, and no heavy lifting as in weight lifting.

That does not imply, however, that riders should simply ignore these muscle groups or that these muscles will not develop by riding a bike. In fact, strong arms and shoulders can make riding much easier and more pleasant. By allowing a rider to grip the handlebars tightly, for instance, strong arm muscles can help cyclists maintain their balance. Sturdy shoulders and arms also help cushion the rest of the

Strong arms and shoulders help a cyclist maintain overall balance, climb a steep incline, and steer on rough terrain.

body against rough spots on the road. "Cycling tends to build muscular endurance in your arms," writes Brian Willett on the website the Nest, "as these muscles are engaged in maintaining a static position to support your body against bumps and curves in the course."[22]

Arm and shoulder strength thus plays a role in all kinds of cycling, from indoor track races to slow-paced rides along flat, paved roadways. It is especially useful, however, in three situations. One is riding uphill, especially on a steep slope. Most riders pull upward on the handlebars as they make their way up the road or the trail. As Marianne McGinnis describes it in an article for *Bicycling* magazine, "you use your shoulders and related muscles to pull yourself up hills."[23] The biceps, which are the muscles located in the upper arms, are especially important for this purpose, and extensive hill work can help develop those muscles.

The second situation in which strong arms and shoulders are useful is in riding with so-called aerobars—handlebars designed to be gripped well below the shoulder level. These handlebars, which include long pads for the forearms, are often found on road bikes built for serious cyclists. The design pushes the rider into a highly aerodynamic position in which the rider's head and shoulders are tucked down, lowering wind resistance. Because the body is so low and so far forward, much of the rider's weight is resting on the forearms. This tends to strengthen the tricep muscles, which are located in the back of the upper arm.

Riding on a mountain bike trail is the third situation in which strong arms and shoulders are useful. Powerful arm and shoulder muscles are helpful in steering through the tight and sudden turns common on hillsides; riders need strength to turn the handlebars quickly and decisively so they can make these turns as smooth and accurate as possible. Shoulders and arms also help riders guide the bicycle past rocks and other obstacles. In fact, mountain bikers often jerk their handlebars up to help them over ditches and roots.

Powerful Legs

While strong arms and shoulders are important to cyclists, the lower body is far more vital in cycling. As one cycling coach points out, "going quick on a bike . . . is about leg speed and leg strength."[24] The legs, after all, are what turn the pedals, and the pedals make the bicycle go forward. The more powerfully and rapidly the pedals rotate, the faster the bike moves. Without powerful legs, a cyclist will find cycling difficult.

However, cycling does not develop or rely upon all leg muscles equally. The muscles associated most closely with cycling are the quadriceps, or quads—extensions of the knee joint located at the front of the upper leg. Bicycle pedals move as a direct result of the up-and-down motion of the quadriceps, and the quadriceps are the muscles that, more

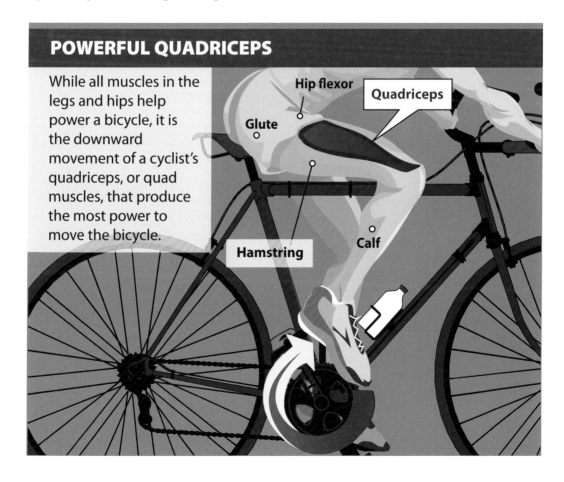

POWERFUL QUADRICEPS

While all muscles in the legs and hips help power a bicycle, it is the downward movement of a cyclist's quadriceps, or quad muscles, that produce the most power to move the bicycle.

Hip flexor

Quadriceps

Glute

Hamstring

Calf

than any other, drive the rest of the system. "When a cyclist pushes down on the pedals," says physical therapist Mike Aunger, "it is mostly from the action of the quadriceps that power is produced and transferred into the rear wheel."[25]

In fact, the quadriceps muscles are remarkably well developed in many cyclists. Sir Chris Hoy, a British track cyclist who retired in 2013 with six Olympic gold medals in cycling, is just one of several well-known riders who has enormous thighs, thanks in large part to the constant working of the quadriceps muscles. Eric Heiden, an American speed skater who won five gold medals in speed skating at the 1980 Olympics and later became a cycling champion, had thighs "so massive," one *New York Times* reporter notes, "he needed size 38 pants even though his waist measured only 32 inches."[26] Robert Förstemann, a German track cyclist who won a bronze medal in team track cycling at the 2012 Olympics, has a waist size that is smaller than either of his thighs; he is informally known as Mr. Thigh or Quadzilla among cycling fans and his fellow competitors.

Other Important Muscles

While the quadriceps are the most-worked muscles in the thigh, they are not the only ones a cyclist uses. The hamstring muscles, located in the back of the thigh, are also essential in cycling. Specifically, the hamstrings (sometimes called "hams" for short) are used in the recovery, or the upstroke, in pedaling. Richard Ballantine and Richard Grant, authors of the book, *The Ultimate Bicycle Book*, explain, "As you push down with the quads at the top of your thigh and extend your leg, the hams underneath contract to bring the leg back up to complete the circular pedaling motion."[27] A rider with weak hamstrings cannot pedal as efficiently as one whose hamstrings are stronger.

While cyclists rely on the muscles of the upper leg, they do not make much use of the muscles of the lower leg. For cyclists the lower leg is mainly an extension of the upper leg; they only use the knee and the foot. The knee is the joint that connects the upper leg muscles to the lower leg, so a weak knee can limit the amount of power that riders can transfer from their thighs to the pedals, while a strong knee can

Although cyclists rely upon strong quadriceps muscles to propel their ride, other muscles, including the hamstrings and glutes, also contribute to power and balance.

ensure that all the strength of the upper leg is used to move the bicycle forward. Feet, similarly, can be used to improve performance. This is especially true of serious cyclists, who often ride with their toes encased in clips that keep them firmly on the pedals. Riders can pull up on the pedals with their feet during the recovery part of the pedal rotation, adding a little extra power to their ride.

Several other muscles are used to a lesser degree in cycling. These include the gluteal muscles, also known as the glutes. These muscles, which come in a group of three, are in the rider's buttocks. Like the quadriceps, the glutes are quite powerful. Indeed, they supplement the strength of the quadriceps in making the pedals go around. They also help the cyclist in staying comfortably in the seat and in maintaining his or her balance during a ride.

Finally, cyclists also rely on their core muscles. These muscles are located in the abdomen, back, hips, and neck. They are valuable because they keep the rider upright, stable, and balanced. Having strong, well-toned core muscles can help a rider go somewhat faster, but having core muscles that are relatively weak can slow a cyclist down considerably.

Recumbent Bicycles

The word *recumbent* means "lying down," and a recumbent bicycle allows the rider to do exactly that. On a recumbent bicycle, riders do not perch on a seat the way they do on a standard road or mountain bike. Instead, they lean back on a seat that is only a foot or so above the road. Recumbent bike seat shapes and sizes vary, but they are generally quite different than a typical bike saddle. For example, some recumbent bikes use a sling-shaped seat to allow the rider to recline comfortably. In all cases there is some form of a back rest on which the rider reclines. The pedals are not positioned below the rider's legs but are in front of the rider instead. And instead of pushing the pedals up and down, recumbent riders push the pedals back and forth.

A recumbent bicycle can take some getting used to, but its design is sound. The rider and bike are both positioned very low to the ground, allowing for a correspondingly low center of gravity. Thus, the bicycle is much more stable than a standard road or mountain bike. The low profile of the recumbent also makes it more aerodynamic than most other bikes. The recumbent encounters much less air as it moves along the road, so air resistance slows the bike less than it does taller bikes.

Finally, the rider can bring more power to bear when pedaling a recumbent than other bicycles. By leaning back, the cyclist can fill her lungs more easily with air, expanding lung capacity; moreover, it is easier to translate the back-and-forth pedaling motion of a recumbent into forward speed than the up-and-down pedaling movement of a standard road or mountain bike. Not surprisingly, bicycle speed records typically belong to recumbents.

Body Systems

In addition to various muscles, cyclists also rely on their body systems. A body system is a group of organs that work together to accomplish certain functions. The intestines, stomach, and esophagus, for example, are all part of the digestive system, which converts food into usable energy for the rest of the body. Other important body systems include the immune system, which helps keep the body healthy; the reproductive system, which allows the body to reproduce

The cardiovascular and pulmonary systems, which include the heart, lungs, veins, arteries, and blood, work together to keep the body oxygenated, particularly during physical exercise.

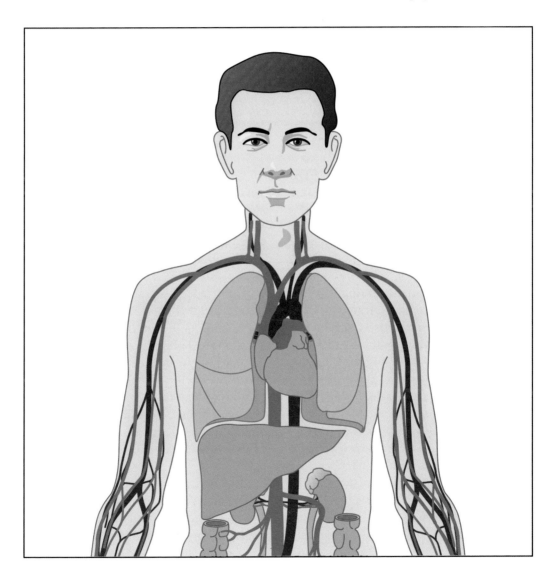

(have babies); and the nervous system, which functions as a communication network between the brain and the rest of the body.

All body systems are of value to cyclists, but two are of particular importance. These are the cardiovascular, or circulatory, system and the pulmonary system, also called the respiratory system. The cardiovascular system consists of the heart and the blood vessels. As the heart beats, it pumps oxygen-rich blood into every part of the body, providing it with the oxygen it needs. The pulmonary system, in turn, regulates breathing; its central organ is the lungs, which take oxygen from the air and bring it into the body. By mixing the oxygen from the lungs into the blood pumped by the heart, the cardiovascular and respiratory systems work together to permit and promote physical activity.

Two-Sport Athletes

Many athletes excel at high levels of competition in more than one sport. In the early 1900s American Jim Thorpe was an Olympic medalist in track who later went on to play professional baseball and football. In the mid–twentieth century, American Babe Didrikson Zaharias dominated women's golf and track, along with several other sports. In the 1980s and early 1990s American Bo Jackson played professional football and baseball.

Some of the most successful two-sport athletes have been cyclists, and the second sport for many of them was speed skating—a sport with which bicycling would seem to have little in common. Even though speed skating is a winter sport performed on blades and cycling is a summer sport performed on wheels, the two have more in common than many people may know. Like cycling, speed skating is a highly aerobic sport that requires plenty of lung power and strong slow-twitch muscles. Similarly, both sports are low-impact activities that emphasize lower-body strength and work the muscles of the thigh heavily. Indeed, speed skaters often include bicycling as part of their overall fitness program.

Athletes who reached the pinnacle of both sports include American Eric Heiden, who became a professional cyclist after winning five speed-skating medals in the 1980 Olympic Games; Canadian Clara Hughes, who followed two Olympic cycling medals with four in skating; and German Christa Luding-Rothenburger, who won medals in both the summer and winter Olympics in 1988.

Oxygen increases physical performance by impacting certain muscles in the body. These muscles are often called slow-twitch muscles; they constitute about half the body's muscles. Slow-twitch muscles use oxygen to generate a type of fuel called adenosine triphosphate, or ATP for short. This fuel causes the muscles to contract slowly and continuously (slow twitching), giving power to the body. The relatively slow and extended contractions mean that these muscles do not fatigue easily, which in turn means that they can power the body for many hours.

Aerobic Sports and Activities

Sports and activities in which athletes and participants are in motion more or less constantly over a lengthy period of time are called aerobic sports and aerobic activities. Aerobic sports include cycling, long-distance running, and long-distance swimming. Aerobic activities can include canoeing, hiking, roller-skating, and any other athletic activity that involves few, if any, rest breaks. Athletes in aerobic sports rely on a steady amount of oxygen in order to succeed.

Strong respiratory and circulatory systems are therefore vital for success in aerobic sports, such as cycling. The more air a cyclist's lungs can take in, the more oxygen will be available to act on slow-twitch muscles; this means that powerful lungs are important to cyclists. Similarly, the more blood the heart can pump in a minute, the more oxygen will be transported throughout the body to produce ATP, making a durable heart valuable in cycling as well. As the body transports oxygen through the bloodstream, then, ATP allows a rider to move forward at a high rate of speed. Better yet, as more oxygen is added to the body through breathing, it creates more ATP, which continues to keep the body going forward. As long as breathing remains strong and regular, progress will continue.

Cycling can increase the body's cardiovascular capacity, enabling the heart to become more efficient, lowering the resting pulse rate, and improving the circulatory system's efficiency. The aerobic demand of cycling, however, means that a rider must have a decent cardiovascular system before beginning to ride.

A cyclist stops to check her heart rate monitor during a ride. As an aerobic activity, cycling elevates the heart rate and increases the amount of oxygen taken into the body.

Anaerobic Sports and Activities

The opposite of aerobic sports and activities are anaerobic sports and activities, which use less oxygen or none at all and are characterized by sudden bursts of intense muscular activity. Anaerobic sports include football and tennis; anaerobic activities include bowling and jumping rope. They rely on so-called fast-twitch muscles, which contract much more quickly and for much less time than slow-twitch muscles. When muscles are worked hard in anaerobic activity, lactic acid stored inside the muscles provides a sudden burst of power. Once the acid has been used up, however—a process that generally takes less than two minutes—it cannot be immediately regenerated; lactic acid needs time to rebuild itself.

Cycling is not typically considered an anaerobic sport. However, track cyclists who ride very short distances do require fast-twitch muscles. Even amateur riders who cycle mainly for fun often enjoy the feeling of riding as hard as they possibly can for a few hundred yards—another example of fast-twitch muscles in use.

Because cycling does not put much stress on joints and muscles, it is an ideal low-impact activity for people with skeletal pain.

Low-Impact Exercise

Riding a bicycle is especially popular as exercise, and unlike other forms of exercise, such as running and walking, cycling is very low-impact. While running or walking, a person's feet are repeatedly impacting the ground. This stresses the bones and muscles, especially of the lower leg and the knee. Cycling, therefore, is a better choice for people with bone density issues or skeletal pain.

All bicycle riders, from amateurs to professional cyclists, rely on essentially the same body systems and muscles to help their bicycle move forward at an appropriate pace. The leg muscles, especially the quadriceps, and the cardiovascular and respiratory systems are of particular value to a cyclist, but other parts of the body, from the shoulder muscles to the feet, are important too.

CHAPTER 5

Nutrition, Training, and Injuries

Bicyclists can be serious athletes. The men's road cycling race in the 2012 Olympic Games in London, England, was 156 miles (251km). The winner, Alexander Vinokourov from Kazakhstan, finished the race in five hours and forty-five minutes. Similarly, in sprint cycling, in which riders go as quickly as possible around an oval track, competitors often reach speeds in excess of 40 miles per hour (64kmh), faster than cars are allowed to travel in most urban areas. While the distances in these races are not great, the speeds achieved require remarkable power. An untrained cyclist would be left far behind in these competitions by a professional cyclist. "While you [a typical recreational rider] may have mad cycling skills," writes journalist Jeannine Stein, "chances are you don't have what it takes to compete against . . . the best racers in the world."[28]

Professional cyclists have better-than-average strength, excellent cardiovascular fitness, and overall good health. Still, no athlete is talented enough to become a great cyclist without an enormous amount of practice. And even cyclists who do not have the physical gifts to be great riders can still improve their skills through training. Any rider, at any skill level, can become faster and stronger by following sensible rules of training and diet.

Nutrition

Proper nutrition is essential for professional cyclists. There are foods that can increase basic health, help add muscle, or provide extra bursts of energy. While there is debate

Vegetables and other nutritious foods are at the center of a serious cyclist's diet.

about the overall nutritional value of many foods, proper nutrition can have an impressive effect on the performance of virtually all cyclists. In an article on Roadcycler .com Tyler Cooper writes, "You will be astonished at what impact the proper diet will have on your cycling."[29]

The principles of nutrition are straightforward. To work, grow, and play, every human body requires nutrients, such as salt, protein, fat, iron, and vitamin A, which are found in various foods and drinks. Different foods contain different amounts of these nutrients. While all foods contain nutrients, not all nutrients are equally helpful in building a strong and healthy body. Nutritionists typically recommend avoiding or at least limiting high-fat and high-sugar foods, for example, and concentrating instead on vegetables, fruits, and basic grains that contain vitamins and minerals.

Nutrients are perhaps the main concern when choosing what foods to eat, but they are by no means the only consideration. Another important quality of foods is how many calories they have. Calories are not themselves a nutrient; rather, they are a measure of the energy value of a food. High-calorie foods, such as cake, and starchy foods, such as sweet potatoes, provide lots of energy to people who eat them; low-calorie foods, such as celery, provide much less. In early hunter-gatherer societies in which food was not always plentiful, high-calorie foods were useful in staving off starvation; but in modern society the food supply is much more consistent and too many calories can be a problem. Too many calories can cause people to gain too much weight, which in turn leads to significant health problems.

Carbohydrates

Carbohydrates are of particular interest to cyclists. Often known as carbs for short, carbohydrates come in two varieties: simple and complex. Simple carbohydrates include fruit, honey, and table sugar. The body quickly breaks these foods down into glucose, a type of sugar that provides energy. The body then distributes the glucose to the muscles. Eating simple carbohydrates can provide a rush of energy, which can be helpful when a cyclist is tired. Unfortunately the

Alberto Contador of Spain prepares to eat a banana mid-race in order to fuel his body with carbohydrates during the 2007 Tour de France.

glucose obtained by eating them is quickly used up, resulting in suddenly low levels of glucose that cause people to feel tired and weak.

Complex carbohydrates, which include starches, such as potatoes; some types of beans; and whole grains, are also made of glucose. Unlike simple carbs, however, the molecular structure of complex carbohydrates is much more sophisticated. This means that the body requires more time to break them down into glucose. "Complex carbohydrates go through a number of metabolic processes," writes Chris Sidwells in his book, *Complete Bike Book*. "[Their] energy is released at a slow, steady rate."[30] The slow rate of transformation means that complex carbs are not an especially good source of immediate energy. It also means that people who eat them avoid the sudden lows that come after eating lots of processed sugar or other simple carbs. Eating complex carbs has another advantage, especially for a rider who is going a long distance: The energy is available for use a little at a time, so there is always energy being produced when the cyclist needs it.

Both recreational and professional cyclists take carbohydrates into consideration before a ride, and many of them attempt to consume exactly the right combination of carbs. Sidwells advises that before a ride, cyclists should "eat a combination of complex carbohydrates, such as cereals with skim milk, pasta, [or] rice." Doing so, he says, will give the body sufficient reserves of carbohydrates, which will then be processed into glucose throughout the ride, providing energy as needed. Eating while riding is important as well. "During the ride," Sidwells explains, "eat a combination of simple and

Junk Food and Ultradistance Riding

For many nutritionists as well as cyclists, the first rule of establishing a healthy diet is simple: limit junk food as much as possible. While chips, ice cream, and brownies may taste good, they are not generally good for the body. High in saturated fat and high in calories, they provide little nutritional value, narrow blood vessels, increase body weight, and stress the heart and lungs.

The main exception to this general principle involves extreme long-distance riders, often known as randonneurs. These athletes routinely ride 125 miles (201km) or more in a day, often for many days in a row, and they may also ride through a twenty-four-hour period with

only occasional rest breaks. These riders require so many calories to keep going that they are encouraged to eat more or less whatever they want. One randonneur describes his intake of food before a particularly intense ride as consisting of "a Spanish omelette and bacon, bananas, a sausage and pepperoni pizza, ham and cheese sandwiches, chicken and cheese sandwiches, ice cream, mushroom soup, [and] french fries." He needed every one of the calories these foods provided to complete the 625-mile (1,006km) journey.

Quoted in Kent Peterson. "What Long Distance Cyclists Really Eat." Kent's Bike Blog, October 26, 2009. http://kentsbike.blogspot.com/2009/10/what-long-distance-cyclists-really-eat.html.

complex carbohydrates. These might include cakes and candies, sports drinks and bars [and] bananas."[31] The complex carbs add to the steady supply of energy; the simple carbs allow for bursts of speed if and when the amount of glucose dwindles and the rider begins to tire.

Protein

A mountain biker takes a break to eat a protein bar so that she can maintain her energy level during her ride.

Protein is also essential to cyclists. Proteins are most commonly found in animal products, such as meat, poultry, seafood, and eggs. Nuts and soybeans are good sources of protein too. Just as the body breaks carbohydrates down into glucose, the body breaks protein down into substances called amino acids. Amino acids repair body tissues, increase immunity to disease, and help to build muscles. Since the body cannot store protein for long, it is important for people to ingest at least some protein every day. Without protein the

human body will lose strength rapidly and eventually die.

Proteins are most important to athletes who participate in power-based sports, such as weight lifting, throwing the discus, and football. Athletes in these sports require enormous strength to compete and may ingest massive amounts of protein, often through supplements, such as protein shakes, to develop the musculature they need. Cyclists, for the most part, do not need so much protein; the only real exceptions are sprinters, track riders who need well-developed muscles to race at top speed for several hundred yards.

Still, doctors and nutritionists advise all cyclists, not just sprinters, to get plenty of protein. Not only does protein offer muscle strengthening and body repair, but it also has other benefits. In her book, *Every Woman's Guide to Cycling*, Selene Yeager writes, "On long rides your brain and muscles use protein as supplemental fuel." Summing up advice from nutritionists, she adds that "endurance athletes like cyclists should eat a minimum of 0.5 grams of protein for every pound of body weight, or about 70 grams for a 140-pound woman."[32]

Saturated and Unsaturated Fats

Fats are important for cyclists too, as they are for all people. Without fats, the body cannot absorb certain essential vitamins; a lack of these vitamins can bring about sickness and even death. Like carbohydrates, fats are often subdivided into categories, including saturated fats and unsaturated fats. Saturated fats are usually, although not always, in solid form at room temperature; these include butter, margarine, the fat of a steak or a pork chop, and shortening. Most nutritionists recommend avoiding these fats when possible, and that advice applies just as much to cyclists as to the general public. "Saturated fats slow the metabolism, encourage the build-up of cholesterol, and are linked with high blood pressure and heart disease,"[33] explains Sidwells.

FINISH LINE
550
Number of calories a 200-pound man will burn riding a bicycle at 11 miles per hour for an hour

Heart Rates

The best way to improve heart function is to exercise. Most trainers recommend keeping the heart rate within a certain range while exercising in order to improve heart function. A doctor or a professional trainer can recommend the proper heart rate range for a given person by taking into account the person's age, weight, fitness level, and overall health profile. This range elevates the heart rate above the normal resting rate but keeps it from going too high, which can be unhealthy for the person exercising. In most cases, it is not wise to train for long at the heart's maximum possible rate, as it puts unnecessary strain on the heart and can potentially cause a heart attack. Trainers typically suggest setting a maximum heart rate for exercise by using the following formula: ¾ x [220 – age]

To use the formula, an athlete inserts his or her age and completes the math. For example, for a 20-year-old athlete the formula is ¾ x [220 – 20]. Calculating the math results in a maximum heart rate of 150 (¾ x 200).

Professional bike racers and other very experienced riders may sometimes choose to exercise at a higher heart rate because they have conditioned their bodies, over many years, to perform at this level. For most amateurs, however, regular exercise that brings the heart rate above the maximum heart rate formula is not sustainable and not healthy.

Unsaturated fats, which are usually in liquid form at room temperature, include olive oil and peanut oil, as well as the oils in foods such as salmon, tofu, and nuts. Unlike saturated fats, unsaturated fats are associated with lower risks of diseases, notably diabetes, cardiac problems, and high cholesterol. Unsaturated fats can also provide fuel for the body, especially when people are engaged in low-level continuous activity, including cycling. Most nutritionists, therefore, recommend that people consume unsaturated fats instead of saturated fats. Yeager explains that "for optimal performance" cyclists should "aim to eat about 30% of [their] calories from healthy [unsaturated] fats."[34]

Lots of Water

Although riders should pay close attention to what they eat if they want to ride well, paying attention to how much water they drink is even more critical. During any physical activity, such as cycling, the human body is constantly losing water. Some is lost to sweat; some is used by muscles and other body parts. All the water that is lost must be replaced and the sooner the better. Dehydration, or lack of water, is a significant problem for cyclists who neglect to take in enough liquid while riding. "Always carry water with you," advises Sidwells, "and do not wait until you are thirsty before you drink, since this means you are already dehydrated."[35]

A cyclist stops for a drink of water in order to keep his body hydrated during his ride.

Many people think dehydration only occurs on hot days, but this is not true. While a hot day can certainly help dehydration occur faster, any physical activity causes the body to lose water and people often do not realize how quickly they can become dehydrated. Dehydration can be extremely dangerous, leading to unconsciousness and death, so drinking water should always be a part of any physical activity.

Training

In addition to eating a healthy diet and drinking plenty of water, cyclists should engage in training appropriate for them. An athlete's overall physical condition, time available for practice, and ultimate goals all affect the type and intensity of training he or she chooses. For casual riders, advice regarding training is often very simple: Just ride. "The thought of riding 25 or, heaven forbid, 50 miles may sound intimidating," writes cycling expert Howard Stone in his book, *25 Bicycle Tours in the Hudson Valley*, "[but] anyone in normal health can do it . . . if you get into a little bit of shape first, which you can accomplish painlessly by riding at a leisurely pace for an hour or two several times a week for about 3 weeks."[36] For more competitive cyclists, however, simply riding is not enough. These riders typically follow a precise training program, one that is tailored specifically for them.

A training program for a competitive cyclist might include regular rides of forty-five to ninety minutes five days a week, with two days off for resting and recharging. Most trainers advise that cyclists pedal at about 70 percent of their maximum heart rate most of the time, riding on a mixture of hills, rolling land, and flat roads. To develop anaerobic capacity, riders aim for three or more sudden bursts of speed during these rides, each lasting about a minute.

Over time a cyclist's body will adjust to the demands of his or her training program, and as that happens, the trainer will make adjustments in the training. Changes may include increasing the number of high-intensity bursts during rides, reducing the number of rest days, and raising the heart rate when possible. All changes in training will depend on the rider's specific needs and vulnerabilities. Sidwells advises that "after a few races or long-distance challenges,"[37] cyclists should focus on their weak points during training.

Injuries

Even the best training program cannot eliminate the possibility of injuries in cycling. Injuries are, in fact, common among racers and other serious riders. In 2011 alone thirty-eight thousand bicycle-related injuries were reported in the United States. However, most experts believe that for every reported injury there are ten more that are unreported. If true, this means that the true number of bicycle injuries in 2011 was over four hundred thousand.

The most common bicycle injuries are the result of accidents, the consequences of which can be extremely unpleasant.

A mother makes sure her daughter puts on her helmet before taking a bike ride. Helmets can prevent the rider from sustaining a serious head injury in a fall.

FINISH LINE

During his cycling career, American Tyler Hamilton broke a shoulder, an elbow, several ribs, a wrist, his nose, his back, multiple fingers, and one of his collarbones twice.

The forward momentum of a bike and rider is powerful, and it becomes more powerful as speed increases. Even if the bike hits an obstacle and stops moving, the rider will continue moving forward. Being flung from a bike at any speed can result in bruises, scrapes, broken bones, and other injuries. "I went over the handlebars and landed squarely on my spine," recalls American racer Tyler Hamilton of a crash he suffered during the Tour de France, a major annual cycling race in France. "I hadn't just hurt my back, I had damaged it."[38]

No one can completely eliminate the possibility of an accident, but experts do suggest ways to limit the risk. One is for cyclists to ride with caution. That means recognizing the potential hazards and responding accordingly—riding more slowly in the rain, for instance, or paying closer attention to traffic. Another is to wear protective gear, such as a helmet to guard against head injuries, gloves and wrist guards to help avoid hand and arm injuries, and reflective clothing to aid others in seeing them in the dark. "My cycling helmet saved my life,"[39] writes British cyclist Alex Lom in an article for the *Telegraph*, a London newspaper.

Cycling itself is not known for causing injuries. Unlike weight lifting or baseball, it does not unduly tax the arms, shoulders, and back, and unlike running, there is no repeated impact with the ground and, therefore, no special stress on the legs. The legs are, however, the most vulnerable part of the body for cyclists. Trying to pedal too hard can put enormous stress on the knees and to a lesser extent the hips. As bicycle enthusiast Sheldon Brown puts it, cyclists "run a higher risk of muscle stress and joint damage"[40] if they have to push the pedals exceptionally hard. The best advice for avoiding this problem is to downshift into a lower gear. The distance traveled with each pedal rotation may drop, but pedaling will be much easier and will cause a lot less pain for the rider.

Cycling is easy enough that almost anyone in reasonable physical condition can do it. Even a person who is out of shape can benefit enormously by following basic nutritional guidelines, adopting a training program, and avoiding injury. By fueling the body properly and developing muscles appropriately, any cyclist can improve his or her speed and stamina.

CHAPTER 6

Performance-Enhancing Drugs

The Tour de France is the most famous bicycle race in the world. The competitors are all men (as of 2013 there is no equivalent race for women), and they race nearly every day for about three weeks on a route that takes them all around France, and occasionally into nearby countries. The race involves punishing climbs in the Alps and Pyrenees—mountain ranges that extend into France—along with long-distance flat stages requiring the riders to cover as much as 140 miles (225km) in a single day. The entire route typically extends about 2,200 miles (3,541km). Only the very best and physically fit riders finish the race.

Except during World War I (1914–1918) and World War II (1939–1945), the Tour de France has been held every year since its inception in 1903. Despite the difficulties of the course, multiple riders finished the race each time. Yet official records show that from 1999 to 2005 there was no winner of the Tour de France. Even though American cyclist Lance Armstrong crossed the finish line in each of those races with the shortest elapsed time and was originally declared the winner, he is no longer recognized as finishing first. Several years after his last victory, officials determined that Armstrong had used drugs to enhance his performance in the races. Because many other cyclists in those races also used drugs, cycling officials decided not to elevate the ranking of any of the runners-up. Instead, they declared the winner position for all seven races to be officially vacant.

The specific drugs taken by Armstrong and other leading competitors of the time are designed to improve cyclists' speed, strength, and endurance. Known as performance-enhancing drugs or PEDs, these drugs increase the body's ability to do work efficiently and for a long period of time. PEDs give athletes an unfair advantage in competition, and this is why the International Cycling Union, the governing body for cycling, bans the use of PEDs.

Doping and Cycling

Doping, which is the use of PEDs by athletes to improve their performance, is, unfortunately, not new to cycling. In fact, with the single exception of weight lifting, which has experienced what one commentator describes as "one doping violation after another,"[41] cycling has been impacted by PEDs more than any other sport—considerably more even than baseball, football, or track. As early as 1886, soon after the development of bicycle racing, there were accusations that certain British riders were trying to artificially increase their lung capacity by taking nitroglycerin, a substance used to treat shortness of breath by helping to open airways. Just ten years later trainer and coach James "Choppy" Warburton was banned from the sport for life after several of his cyclists died suddenly, possibly of poisoning from ingesting performance-enhancing substances.

During the first half of the twentieth century, chemists began to isolate and develop substances that could significantly increase an athlete's strength or endurance, though few of these were approved for use in competition. With doping becoming more sophisticated over the years, PED use became more common among cyclists. At the 1960 Olympics in Rome, Italy, Danish cyclist Knud Jensen experienced heatstroke, collapsed, and hit his head during the road race. He died later the same day from injuries to his brain. Blood tests done at the hospital during his treatment revealed that he had been using amphetamines, stimulants that improve athletic performance and may also increase

American Lance Armstrong, a seven-time winner of the Tour de France, was one of many top cyclists whose achievements were marred by their use of performance-enhancing drugs.

strength. In an interview in 1965 Jacques Anquetil, a French cyclist and winner of the Tour de France in 1957, 1961, 1962, 1963, and 1964, admitted that he used drugs when competing and then said, "Leave me in peace, everybody takes dope [performance-enhancing drugs]."[42] In 1967 Tom Simpson, an English cyclist, collapsed during the Tour de France and died later the same day at a hospital. Simpson's official cause of death was heart failure due to dehydration and heat exhaustion. The autopsy also revealed that he had amphetamines in his system.

Through the 1960s there were few good ways to determine if an athlete was doping. In the early 1970s, though, it became standard for athletes to be tested for PED use at the Olympics and other important competitions, with those who failed being subject to penalties such as suspensions, lifetime bans from competitions, and loss of titles already won. During the 1970s, 1980s, and early 1990s, some of the biggest names in cycling failed drug tests. They included Belgian Eddy Merckx, considered by some to be the greatest cyclist ever; Frenchman Laurent Fignon, a two-time winner of the Tour de France; and Sean Kelly of Ireland, believed by many to be the greatest cyclist of the 1980s.

In addition to the riders who were caught, other cyclists of the 1970s to the early 1990s were suspected of using PEDs as well. Many of these riders used drugs that could not easily be detected by standard drug tests, however, so their drug use could not be proven while they were active. Following their retirement from cycling, though, a number of these riders have admitted extensive doping. Most observers now believe that successful cyclists from that time period were more likely to be on drugs than not.

And regardless of the situation in 1975 or 1985, there seems little question that PED use had become endemic within cycling by the late 1990s. More and more cyclists were either being caught by drug tests or were admitting, at least in private, that they were taking banned substances. Since 2000, in addition to Armstrong, luminaries such as Floyd Landis and Tyler Hamilton of the United States, Ivan Basso of Italy, Jan Ullrich of Germany, and Michael Rasmussen of Denmark have all been disqualified from competitions or given multiyear suspensions for PED use.

A Systemic Problem

Until about 2006, however, cycling coaches, trainers, and national foundations widely disregarded the rules by encouraging cyclists to use PEDs. In 1997, for example, the doctor for the U.S. Postal Service race team advised team member Scott Mercier to take anabolic steroids, a common PED. If Mercier was caught with the pills, the doctor told him, he

should simply say they were vitamins. Mercier refused and
walked away from cycling for good. "Anybody could see the
decision had been made at the top,"[43] he said later. In other
words, the suggestion to take drugs had really come from
team officials.

Mercier's experience was not unusual. In 1998 in France
police officers stopped a car belonging to the Festina cycling
team (Festina is the watch manufacturer that sponsored the
team) during the Tour de France. The car contained hun-
dreds of bottles of PEDs, many of them not only banned in
cycling but also illegal in France, along with syringes and
other doping equipment. Police arrested the driver of the
car. Festina's team doctor and other team officials said they
knew nothing of the driver's activities and claimed that no
one on the team was doping. Few observers believed them,
and several days later the team's director admitted that the
team was engaged in systematic doping.

French authorities questioned Festina's riders, trainers, and team officials, seeking answers. They locked Swiss rider Alex Zülle in a prison cell overnight and grilled him about his use of PEDs. They also imprisoned several doctors. The scandal quickly spread to other teams: Festina was not the only team providing its riders with PEDs and instructions to use them. Team doctors and officials quickly got rid of the evidence. "Teams were frantically flushing thousands of dollars' worth of pharmaceuticals down the toilets of buses, RVs, and hotels,"[44] recalls Hamilton. In the end authorities were unable to prove much, but they had revealed a connection between cycling and PEDs for everyone to see, and race officials expelled Festina from the Tour de France.

The Price of PED Use

Drug testing in sports is enormously expensive. Sports officials must constantly administer urine tests and sometimes blood tests to athletes to see if they are taking drugs. At the 2012 Olympics in London, England, officials collected over six thousand separate samples from athletes, each of which had to be tested for over four hundred substances that are formally banned by the International Olympic Committee, the governing body for all Olympic Games. It was an expensive process: Lab costs alone were about 60 million dollars.

Drug use by athletes also reduces confidence in sport results and leads to disaffection among fans and athletes alike. No one wants to see their favorite team or athlete defeated because the opponent cheated. Likewise, many fans are disappointed and angry to find out that their favorite athlete is the one doing the cheating. And even when drug test results are negative, controversies may still rage around famous athletes. American cyclist Lance Armstrong, for example, passed drug test after drug test even while rumors flew wildly that he was doping. In his case, the rumors were true. Whether they are true or not, rumors about any athlete and drug use hurt the integrity of all sports, and make people wonder if games, races, and tournaments are really fair contests.

Steroids, Testosterone, and HGH

Over the years, cyclists have used a wide variety of drugs designed to improve their performance. The best known today are anabolic steroids. These drugs are artificial substances, and their only purpose is to boost muscle growth.

American short-track cyclist Tammy Thomas admitted to using testosterone in order to increase her musculature and give her a competitive edge.

Originally, anabolic steroids were developed for use by the very sick: patients with bone, muscle, and protein deficiencies whose systems needed a boost. In the 1950s some physicians began to wonder what would happen if they gave anabolic steroids to athletes who were already in top condition. It turned out that these athletes developed extra muscle as well, muscle that they could put to good use in competition. By the 1960s steroid use was increasingly common among Olympic athletes, including cyclists.

Steroids affected more than just the athletes' strength. Many cyclists spoke of feeling more deeply competitive when under the influence of anabolic steroids: They wanted not only to win, but they also wanted to annihilate their opponents. Quite a few discovered that using steroids seemed to help them recover from their workouts more quickly. And cyclists frequently found that steroids seemed to help them heal faster after an injury. Since cyclists frequently fall, breaking and spraining wrists, shoulders, collarbones, and more, the possibility of healing more quickly proved to be a major incentive for many riders to take steroids.

Testosterone is another substance that can help build muscle. It is a male hormone, naturally present in the body; it exists to a large degree in men and to a small degree in women. Adding synthetic testosterone—that is, testosterone created in a laboratory—to the testosterone the body makes naturally can increase the musculature of male cyclists. Landis, who was the winner of the 2006 Tour de France until race officials stripped the title from him because of PED use, was found to have used synthetic testosterone. In women testosterone is especially effective since their bodies make relatively little of it and they tend to be less heavily muscled than men. Track cyclist Tammy Thomas is one of many female cyclists who has admitted to using testosterone in an effort to win races.

A number of cyclists have also used human growth hormone (HGH). Like steroids, HGH was once used almost exclusively to help people with recognized medical conditions, such as children who seemed destined to grow up to be extremely short. Again like steroids, HGH was eventually discovered to have an effect on world-class athletes, too. Not only does it build strength, but it also has a particularly powerful effect on healing of injuries and sore muscles, making it a common choice for riders who want to get back on their bike as quickly as they can. Armstrong is one of many cyclists who has admitted to using HGH.

EPO and Blood Boosting

Erythropoietin, or EPO for short, is a hormone that increases the oxygen-carrying capacity of the blood. The human body naturally produces EPO, and its function is to stimulate the production of red blood cells, which are the cells that carry oxygen. Some illnesses, notably a red-blood-cell

Beating Drug Tests

Drug testing frequently fails to identify athletes who are taking performance-enhancing drugs. American cyclist Lance Armstrong, a seven-time winner of the Tour de France, never failed a drug test, but other evidence, such as the testimony of other athletes, later proved that he did take PEDs while competing. In 2012 Tour de France officials removed Armstrong as the winner of all his races. Dozens of other cyclists, who also passed test after test during their careers later admitted to using prohibited drugs. With enormous amounts of money at stake in professional sports, such as prize money for top finishers and money from product endorsements, there is great incentive for teams and riders to find ways to cheat.

Athletes use all kinds of methods to beat the tests and conceal their use of banned substances.

One of these methods is to use new drugs. Scientists working for race teams, especially well-funded ones, are constantly producing new PEDs for which there are no tests yet. Another way athletes cheat is to anticipate when they will be tested; Armstrong dropped out of one race when he found out that he would be tested after completing it. A third way athletes cheat is to ingest chemicals that fool the drug tests. Although testing "can't, and never will, catch everyone," says one Olympic official, officials still try.

Quoted in Pete Axthelm. "Using Chemistry to Get the Gold." *Newsweek*, July 25, 1988, p. 62.

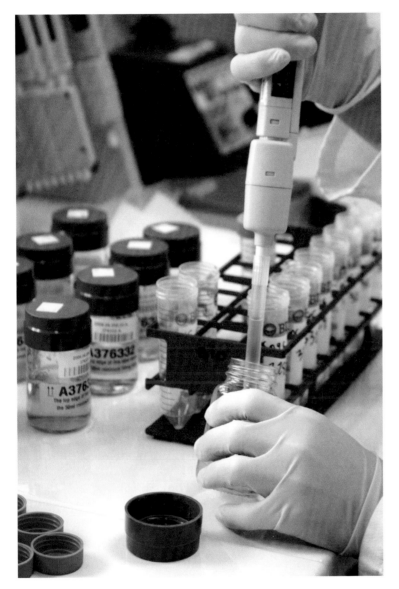

A technician at the French national anti-doping laboratory works with the urine samples of 2008 Tour de France competitors to test them for EPO.

deficiency called anemia, respond well to large doses of EPO. In the 1980s, however, enterprising doctors discovered that injecting extra EPO into healthy cyclists can push even their bodies to make more red blood cells. That in turn improves their blood's ability to carry oxygen and allows them to pedal faster for longer. For a number of years in the late 1980s and into the 1990s, even though EPO was officially banned, there was no blood or urine test that could identify riders who were using the drug, and riders were attracted to EPO for that reason alone.

Blood boosting, or red-cell transfusion, is a method that raises oxygen levels in the body. It is a process that involves injecting red blood cells into the body shortly before an important competition, thus increasing the number of red cells. The cells can come from another person, or they can be drawn from the rider in advance of the contest and stored until needed; the rider's body immediately generates new cells, meaning that the added cells boost the number of red cells above normal levels. While not technically against the rules of cycling until the mid-1980s, cycling officials typically discouraged riders from blood boosting for years. Still, there is little doubt that blood boosting increases a rider's ability to carry oxygen in the blood and can improve performance times and speeds.

An "Arms Race"

Doping has been widespread in cycling for one fundamental reason: PEDs work. Riders who dope gain a noticeable advantage. Mercier found that as more and more of his competitors began taking drugs, particularly EPO, he had more and more trouble keeping up with them. "You get frustrated when your peers are beating your head into the gutter," Mercier explained after he retired. "You're thinking, 'How is this guy suddenly so much better than me?'"[45] Riders who doped, similarly, often speak of a rapid improvement in their ability and a general sense that cycling was suddenly much easier. "You're not wiped out," says Hamilton about being on EPO. "You feel healthy, normal, strong."[46]

The effectiveness of PEDs also led to what Hamilton calls an "arms race between teams."[47] In the 1990s and early 2000s, it was abundantly clear that some teams and countries were supplying their riders with drugs; and just as clearly, whether because it was easier to ignore the behavior, because drugs were somehow a part of cycling culture, or for some other reason, cycling officials did not seemed especially interested in stopping them. Under these circumstances, it was only natural that nondoping teams, tired of having their riders

constantly left behind by opponents under the influence of PEDs, began doping programs of their own. That in turn encouraged the teams that already used drugs to search out even more effective substances or methods to maintain their original advantage, and the cycle continued. Because officials frequently looked the other way when drugs were being taken, cycling gradually became more and more riddled with PEDs.

Not all PEDs are equally effective for all cyclists. Hamilton points out that because everyone has a different metabolism, or rate at which a body processes and uses energy, some riders do not benefit from PEDs as much as others. That is borne out anecdotally. In 1984, shortly before blood boosting was banned, coaches for the U.S. Olympic cycling team

Italian cyclist Riccardo Ricco exits the anti-doping control bus after submitting to a urine test for performance-enhancing drugs during the 2008 Tour de France.

injected a number of riders with stored blood shortly before races. The results were decidedly mixed. Several cyclists became ill, which sharply impacted their performance. "[I] rode the worst I ever rode in my life,"[48] recalls one cyclist. Others, however, won medals, including track cyclist Steve Hegg, who won gold, and road racer Rebecca Twigg, who won silver. The overall effect of the blood boosting was evidently positive—at least as far as winning medals for the United States was concerned—but not all participants benefited equally.

Negative Impacts

While they may improve an athlete's performance, PEDs also have some very negative impacts. In the 1980s and 1990s, as many as eighteen young Belgian and Dutch cyclists died while experimenting with EPO. While extra red blood cells increase the oxygen capacity of the blood, they also make the blood thicker and harder to pump, and the eighteen young riders died, mostly in their sleep, when their hearts proved unable to manage the stress.

Even when drug use does not result in death, it can still have harmful effects on health. Overuse of steroids, for instance, can shrink men's testicles and cause impotence, which is the inability to father children. Injecting blood from strangers can produce bad reactions in otherwise healthy people. Using large amounts of testosterone can improve a female athlete's strength but can also cause her to develop male characteristics, such as male pattern baldness and a deep voice. American track cyclist Tammy Thomas, who tested positive for PEDs twice and was eventually banned from the sport altogether, began to grow facial hair. And PEDs can produce emotional changes. So-called roid rage, in which athletes have sudden angry overreactions, is common in cyclists who take steroids.

Cyclists and other athletes who use PEDs often convince themselves, or are told by their team doctors and other officials, that whatever health damage they suffer from steroids and similar substances is only temporary. In some cases that is absolutely true, and the body returns to normal soon after the athlete stops taking the drug. In other cases, however, the changes are irreversible and will continue through life. They may also lead to further medical problems. "Physically, [Tammy Thomas is] weaker than her elderly parents because of her body's deterioration from long-term doping,"[49] writes journalist Emily Le Coz in the *USA Today* newspaper. Thomas's drug use also left her chronically tired, and she is unable to do much athletically. Thomas is among many former cyclists who wish they had never begun to take PEDs.

The role of PEDs in cycling has changed considerably since Armstrong, Hamilton, Thomas, and their peers were taking them. While few would argue today that not a single professional cyclist uses EPO, steroids, or HGH, there are plenty of signs that the widespread use of PEDs among cyclists has subsided considerably. Well-publicized investigations by governments, athletic foundations, and journalists have made it more difficult for teams and individual riders to evade detection; more thorough drug testing procedures threaten to catch a greater number of users; and many, though not all, of the team doctors and team leaders who helped establish a culture of PEDs are no longer involved in cycling. Hopefully PED use has indeed dropped and will continue to do so in the future.

NOTES

Introduction: The Bicycle

1. Quoted in New York Bicycling Coalition. "March Is Women's (Bike) History Month!" New York Bicycling Coalition, March 7, 2013. www.nybc.net/march-is-womens-bike-history-month.
2. Zap Twin Cities. www.derozap.com/zaptwincities.

Chapter 1: Force, Friction, and Forward Motion

3. Bill Haduch. *Go Fly a Bike!* New York: Dutton, 2004, p. 28.
4. Rick Ashburn. "The Physics of Moving a Bike." Slowtwitch.com, December 26, 2007. www.slowtwitch.com/Tech/The_Physics_of_Moving_a_Bike_163.html.

Chapter 2: Stability, Steering, and Aerodynamics

5. Exploratorium. "The Science of Cycling: Braking & Steering." www.exploratorium.edu/cycling/brakes2.html.

6. Haduch. *Go Fly a Bike!* p. 8.
7. Exploratorium. "The Science of Cycling: Braking & Steering."
8. Exploratorium. "The Science of Cycling: Braking & Steering."
9. Haduch. *Go Fly a Bike!* p. 30.
10. Exploratorium. "The Science of Cycling: Braking & Steering."
11. Sheldon Brown. "Bicycle Coaster Brakes." SheldonBrown.com. http://sheldonbrown.com/coaster-brakes.html.
12. Frank Rowland Whitt and David Gordon Wilson. *Bicycling Science*, 2nd ed. Cambridge: Massachusetts Institute of Technology, 1982, p. 191.
13. Quoted in Exploratorium. "The Science of Cycling: Braking and Steering."

Chapter 3: Basic Bicycle Components

14. Robert Penn. *It's All About the Bike.* New York: Bloomsbury, 2010, p. 15.
15. Whitt and Wilson. *Bicycling Science*, p. 245.
16. Richard Ballantine and Richard Grant. *The Ultimate Bicycle Book.*

London: DK, 1992, p. 58.

17. Quoted in Penn. *It's All About the Bike*, p. 33.

18. Exploratorium. "The Science of Cycling: Frames and Materials." www.exploratorium.edu/cycling/frames2.html.

19. Exploratorium. "The Science of Cycling: Frames and Materials."

20. Ballantine and Grant. *The Ultimate Bicycle Book*, p. 154.

21. Penn. *It's All About the Bike*, p. 8.

Chapter 4: Muscles and Body Systems

22. Brian Willett. "Does Cycling Benefit Muscle Groups?" The Nest. http://woman.thenest.com/cycling-benefit-muscle-groups-13065.html.

23. Marianne McGinnis. "Shoulder the Load." *Bicycling*. www.bicycling.com/training-nutrition/injury-prevention/shoulder-load.

24. Quoted in Greg Bishop. "Thigh-Popping Success on a Bike Lies in the Quads." *New York Times*, August 6, 2012. www.nytimes.com/2012/08/07/sports/olympics/olympic-cyclists-thigh-popping-success-starts-in-quads.html?pagewanted=all&_r=0.

25. Quoted in Tom Eeles. "Cycling Stretches to Prevent Over Use Injuries." SwissRetreat, April 11, 2012. www.swissretreat.com/cycling-stretches.

26. Jeré Longman. "Former Speedskating Champion Heiden Is Staying Close to the Ice." *New York Times*, September 30, 2009. www.nytimes.com/2009/10/01/sports/01heiden.html?pagewanted=all&_r=0.

27. Ballantine and Grant. *The Ultimate Bicycle Book*, p. 19.

Chapter 5: Nutrition, Training, and Injuries

28. Jeannine Stein. "Think You're Tour de France Material? Probably Not." *Los Angeles Times*, July 21, 2011. http://articles.latimes.com/2011/jul/21/news/la-heb-tour-de-france-20110721.

29. Tyler Cooper. "Ride Faster and Longer. Cycling Nutrition 101: Part 1." Roadcycler.com, August 30, 2006. www.roadcycler.com/2006/08/ride-faster-and-longer-cycling-nutrition-101-part-1.

30. Chris Sidwells. *Complete Bike Book*. New York: DK, 2003, p. 148.

31. Sidwells. *Complete Bike Book*, p. 149.

32. Selene Yeager. *Every Woman's Guide to Cycling*. New York: Penguin, 2008, p. 247.

33. Sidwells. *Complete Bike Book*, p. 148.

34. Yeager. *Every Woman's Guide to Cycling*, p. 252.

35. Sidwells. *Complete Bike Book*, p. 149.

36. Howard Stone. *25 Bicycle Tours in the Hudson Valley*. Woodstock, VT: Backcountry, 1996, p. 10.

37. Sidwells. *Complete Bike Book*, p. 154.

38. Quoted in Anthony Tan. "Tyler Tough." Cyclingnews.com, August 14, 2004. http://autobus.cyclingnews.com/road/2004/olympics04/?id=features/aug14tyler_hamilton04.

39. Alec Lom. "My Cycling Helmet Saved My Life." *Telegraph*, March 23, 2009. www.telegraph.co.uk/health/5024212/My-cycling-helmet-saved-my-life.html.

40. Sheldon Brown. "Everything You Wanted to Know About Shifting Your Bicycle's Gears, But Were Afraid to Ask." http://sheldonbrown.com/gears.html.

Chapter 6: Performance-Enhancing Drugs

41. Associated Press. *Weightlifting Still Struggling to Escape Its Sordid History*. ESPN.com, May 16, 2008. http://sports.espn.go.com/espn/wire?section=oly&id=3400027.

42. Quoted in Fiona Carruthers. "Meet Cycling's Freewheeling, Tour de France Winning Defender of Dope." *BRW*, March 3, 2013. http://brw.com.au/p/lifestyle/sport/meet_cycling_freewheeling_tour_de_Qxpkkxei9wJb8X4kQp7zRP.

43. Quoted in Tyler Hamilton and Daniel Coyle. *The Secret Race*. New York: Bantam, 2012, p. 44.

44. Hamilton and Coyle. *The Secret Race*, p. 73.

45. Quoted in Simon Austin. "Lance Armstrong Case Creates an Unlikely Hero." BBC, October 12, 2012. www.bbc.co.uk/sport/0/cycling/19930514.

46. Hamilton and Coyle. *The Secret Race*, pp. 57–58.

47. Hamilton and Coyle. *The Secret Race*, p. 60.

48. Quoted in John Carey. "The Racers' Edge?" *Newsweek*, January 21, 1985, p. 66.

49. Emily Le Coz. "Doping Scandal Haunts Former Cyclist Tammy Thomas." *USA Today*, March 1, 2013. www.usatoday.com/story/sports/cycling/2013/03/01/doping-scandal-haunts-tammy-thomas/1958053.

GLOSSARY

aerodynamics: The study of how air moves, especially around other objects.

air resistance: A force that slows objects when they encounter air or wind.

anabolic steroids: Artificial substances designed to boost muscle growth.

EPO: Short for erythropoietin, a substance that stimulates the body's production of red blood cells.

fatigue-limit stress: Measure of a bike frame's durability.

frame: The network of metal pieces on which the wheels, seat, and pedals of a bicycle are supported.

friction: A force that slows movement through contact between objects.

gravity: A force that exerts a pull on the objects around it.

quadriceps: Muscles located in the front of the thigh.

reciprocating motion: A repetitive movement that produces circular motion.

spoke: A long, thin piece of metal running from the hub of a bicycle wheel to the rim.

truss: A structure built from interlocking triangles.

ultimate tensile stress: Measure of the greatest stress a bike frame can withstand.

Books

Joe Friel. *The Cyclist's Training Bible*. Boulder, CO: Velo, 2009. Information about training methods for cyclists, including but not limited to competitive riders.

Max Glaskin. *Cycling Science: How Rider and Machine Work Together*. Chicago, IL: University of Chicago, 2012. Describes some of the science behind bicycles and how they work; includes information on the muscles used in cycling, the ideal shape of the bicycle frame, and more.

Madeline Goodstein. *Wheels! Science Projects with Bicycles, Skateboards, and Skates*. Berkeley Heights, NJ: Enslow, 2010. This book explains some of the scientific principles behind bicycles; it includes hands-on projects to illustrate these principles.

Bill Haduch. *Go Fly a Bike!* New York: Dutton, 2004. Information about bicycles, the history of bicycles, and how bicycles work. Intended mainly for middle school students.

Tyler Hamilton and Daniel Coyle. *The Secret Race*. New York: Bantam, 2012. Hamilton was a world-class cyclist who became involved in doping. This memoir describes the widespread use of performance-enhancing drugs in the 1990s and early 2000s.

Robert Penn. *It's All About the Bike*. New York: Bloomsbury, 2010. This book describes Penn's efforts to construct an ideal bicycle. It includes lots of information about how bikes are constructed and why their design is so effective.

Chris Sidwells. *Complete Bike Book*. New York: DK, 2003. A well-illustrated volume giving information about types of bicycles, bicycle care and repair, and how bicycles work.

Internet Sources

Pedaling History Bicycle Museum. "A Quick History of Bicycles." www.pedalinghistory.com/PHhistory.html. Focuses on how bicycles have developed through the ages; includes a number of useful illustrations as well as text.

Websites

Bicycling (www.bicycling.com). Bicycling is the website for *Bicycling*, a leading magazine for cyclists. It offers numerous articles and photos about the sport.

Exploratorium (www.exploratorium .edu/cycling). This is the website of the Exploratorium, a science museum in San Francisco, California. It offers an online exhibit on cycling called the Science of Cycling, which explains the science behind the sport.

Slowtwitch (www.slowtwitch.com). This is an online sports magazine offering information about sports, including cycling.

Sports and Drugs (http://sportsanddrugs .procon.org). Offered by ProCon.org, a nonprofit organization that researches controversial issues, this site provides information about performance-enhancing drugs, including drug use by athletes; drug testing; drug use at the Olympics; and the legal, moral, and ethical issues involved in using performance-enhancing drugs.

A

Accidents, 75–76
Adenosine triphosphate, 61
Aerobars, 54
Aerobic sports, 61–62
Aerodynamics, 28, *29*, 30
Air resistance, *21*
    effects, 20–21
    posture, 28, *29*, 30
    recumbent bikes, 58
    wheels, 46
Aluminum frames, 41
Anabolic steroids, 84–85, 90
Anaerobic sports, 63
Anquetil, Jacques, 80
Anthony, Susan B., 9
Arms, *53*, 53–54
Armstrong, Lance, 78–79, *80*, 83, 86
Athletes, two-sport, 60
Aviation, 32

B

Balance, 15, 25–27, 32, 53, 58
Basso, Ivan, 81
Bicycles
    history, 8–9
    types, 10
    See also Components, bicycle

Blood boosting, 88, 89–90
Body systems, 59–63
Brakes, 30–36, *31*, *33*

C

Cadence, 44
Calories, 67, 69, 71
Carbohydrates, 67–70, *68*
Carbon fiber frames, 41
Cardiovascular system, *59*, 60, 61
Center of gravity, 24
Chains, *48*, 48–49, *50*
Circulatory system. *See* Cardiovascular
    system
Cities promoting cycling, 9–10
Coaster brakes, 32–34, *33*
Competetiveness, 85
Complex carbohydrates, 68–70
Components, bicycle, *40*
    brakes, 31–36
    chains, *48*, 48–49
    frames, 37–43, *42*
    gears, 49–51, *50*
    pedals, 46–48, *47*
    spokes, 45–46
    tubes and tires, 18, 31–32, *45*, 46
    wheels, *43*, 43–45
Contact points, 15, 19, 20, 22
Contador, Alberto, 68

Core muscles, 58
Costs
    drug testing, 83
    frames, 41
Cranks, 46–47
Cyclists
    body systems, 59–63
    hydration, 72–74, *73*
    injuries and accidents, 75–76
    low-impact exercise, 64
    muscles, 53–58, 63
    nutrition, *66*, 66–72, *68*, *70*
    physical attributes, 52
    protective gear, *75*, 76
    speed, 65
    training, 74–75
    See also Performance enhancing
        drugs

D
Dehydration, 73–74
Design
    brakes, 31–36
    frames, 41–43, *42*
    history of the bicycle, 8–9
Diamond-shaped frame, 42–43
Diet. *See* Nutrition
Disc wheels, 46
Doping. *See* Performance enhancing
    drugs
Downshifting, 51
Drais, Karl von, 8
Drug tests, 80–81, 83, 86,
    87, *89*
Drugs. *See* Performance enhancing
    drugs
Dunlop, John Boyd, 18

E
Emotional effects of steroid use, 90
Energy, 17, 68–69
Environmental benefits of cycling,
    9–10
Erythropoietin (EPO), 86–88, *87*, 90

F
Fans, 83
Fast-twitch muscles, 63
Fatigue-limit stress, 38
Feet, 57
Festina cycling team, *82*, 82–83
Fignon, Laurent, 81
Fitting methods, bicycle, 39
Flexibility, frame, 39, 41
Force, 12–13, 15–18, 22–23, 48–49
Förstemann, Robert, 56
Frames, 37–43, *38*, *42*
Friction, 13–15, *14*, 18–20, *19*, 22

G
Gears, 49–51, *50*
Gluteal muscles, 55, 57–58
Gravity, 13, 15–18, *16*
Gravity, center of, 24

H
Hamilton, Tyler, 76, 81, 88, 89
Hamstrings, *55*, 56
Handlebars, 25–26, 54
Healing, 85, 86
Health consequences of drug use,
    90–91
Heart rate, 61, 62, *62*, 72

Hegg, Steve, 90
Heiden, Eric, 56, 60
Helmets, *75, 76*
Hoy, Chris, 56
Hughes, Clara, 60
Human growth hormones, 85–86
Hydration, 72–74, *73*

I

Indurain, Miguel, 54
Initial force, 22–23
Injuries, 75–76, 85, 86
International Cycling Union, 79
International Olympic Committee, 83
Intuitive riding, 36
Invention of the bicycle, 8–9

J

Jackson, Bo, 60
Jensen, Knud, 79–80

K

Kelly, Sean, 81
Kinetic energy, 17

L

Lactic acid, 63
Lallement, Pierre, 8
Landis, Floyd, 81, 85
Legs, *55,* 55–56, *57,* 76
Lom, Alex, 76
Low-impact exercise, 63, *63*
Low-pressure areas, 30
Luding-Rothenburger, Christa, 60
Lung capacity, 54, 58

M

Mass, 27, 28
Materials, frame, 40–41
*Mathematical Principles of Natural
    Philosophy* (Newton), 11
Matthes, Ruthie, 36
Mercier, Scott, 81–82, 88
Merckx, Eddy, 81
Metal frames, 40–41
Momentum, 19–20, 27
Motion, Newton's laws of.
    See Newton's laws of motion
Mountain biking, 54
Muscles, *53,* 53–58, *55, 57,* 61, 63

N

Newton's laws of motion, 11–13, *12,*
    25, 28
Nonmetal frames, 41
Nutrition, *66,* 66–72, *68, 70*

O

Olympics, 79–81, 83, 89–90

P

Pedals, 46–48, *47, 48*
Performance enhancing drugs
    erythropoietin, 86–88, *87*
    human growth hormones, 85–86
    pervasiveness, 78–83, 88–89
    steroids, 84–85
Plunger brakes, *31,* 31–32
Popularity of cycling, 8
Posture, 28, *29,* 30
Potential energy, 17

Protective gear, *75*, 76
Protein, *70*, 70–71
Pulmonary system, *59*, 60, 61

Q

Quadriceps, *55*, 55–56

R

Radonneurs, 69
Rasmussen, Michael, 81
Reciprocating motion, 46–48
Recumbent bicycles, 58
Red-cell transfusions, 88
Respiratory system. *See* Pulmonary
    system
Resting heart rate, 61, 62
Ricco, Riccardo, *89*
Rim brakes, *34*, 34–35
Rims, 45
Roid rage, 90

S

Safety, 32, 76
Saturated fats, 71–72
Self-stability, 26
Shoulders, *53*, 53–54
Simple carbohydrates, 67–70, *69*
Simpson, Tom, 80
Sizing methods, bicycle, 39
Skaters, 56, 60
Slopes, *16*, 17–18, 50–51, 54
Slow-twitch muscles, 61, 63
Slowing, 30–36
Speed, 13–15, 28, 30, 44
Speed skaters, 56, 60

Spokes, 45–46
Sprint cycling, 63, 65
Sprockets, 49–50, *50*
Stability, 15, 24–26, *25*,
    43, 44
Steel frames, 41
Steering, 27–28
Steroids, 84–85
    emotional effects of use, 90
Stopping, 30–36
Strength, frame, 43
Strength, physical, 71
Stress
    frames, 38
    wheels, 44
Surface conditions, 18, *19*, 22, *22*

T

Tandem bicycles, 49
Testosterone, 85, 90
Thomas, Tammy, *84*, 85, 90, 91
Tire pressure, 22
Tires, 18, 31–32, *45*, 46
Titanium frames, 41
Tour de France
    Armstrong, Lance, 78–79,
        80, 86
    Festina cycling team, *82*, 82–83
    injuries, 76
    performance enhancing drug use,
        80–81
Training, 74–75
Triangular frame shape, 41–43, *42*
Trusses, *42*, 43
Tubes, *45*, 46
Twigg, Rebecca, 90
Two-sport athletes, 60

U

Ullrich, Jan, 81
Ultimate tensile stress, 38
Ultradistance cycling, 69
Unsaturated fats, 71–72
U.S. Olympic cycling team, 89–90
U.S. Postal Service race team, 81–82

V

Vinokourov, Alexander, 65

W

Warburton, James "Choppy," 79
Water. *See* Hydration

Weight

Weight
    frames, 40, 41
    spokes, 46
    wheels, 44
Weight shifting, 26, 27
Wheels, *43*, 43–45
Wind, 20–21, *21*
Women, 9, 85, 90
Wright, Orville and Wilbur, 32

Z

Zaharias, Babe Didrikson, 60
ZAP Twin Cities program
    (MN), 10
Zülle, Alex, 83

PICTURE CREDITS

Stephen Currie is the author of dozens of books for children and young adults, including *The Olympic Games*, *African American Inventors*, and *Mayan Mythology* for Lucent Books. He is also an educator, who has taught classes from kindergarten to college. Currie enjoys riding his bicycle in the hills—and especially on the flats—of Dutchess County, New York, where he lives.